# My Sister Tatiana, My Brother Ivan

# My Sister Tatiana, My Brother Ivan

## Learning to Know the Soviets

*Helen Bailey, Editor*

BRETHREN PRESS
Elgin, Illinois

# *My Sister Tatiana, My Brother Ivan*

BRETHREN PRESS, 1451 Dundee Avenue,
Elgin, Illinois 60120.

Cover design by Jim Massman; photos by Clyde E. Weaver
Illustrations by Jane Bernhardt

Library of Congress Cataloging-in-Publication Data

My sister Tatiana, my brother Ivan: learning to know the
    Soviets/Helen Bailey, editor.
        146 p.        cm.
        Bibliography: p. 145
        ISBN 0-87178-595-1
        1. Soviet Union—Description and travel—1970- 2. Soviet
    Union—Foreign public opinion, American. 3. Public
    opinion—United States. I. Bailey, Helen.
    DK29.M895 1988
    947.085'4—dc19

Manufactured in the United States of America

*To all those who are weaving
the fabric of peace*

# Acknowledgements

The editor and publisher wish to thank the holders of copyrighted materials for permission to reprint from the following sources:

*Associated Press,* Bureau Chief, Drusic Meniker, for a news item October 1985, "Climbers Stage High-Altitude Summit Meeting."

*Sojourners Magazine,* P.O. Box 29272, Washington, DC 20017, for "Crossing Boundaries," and "The Faces of Olga, Yuri and Volodya."

*Peacework: A New England Peace and Justice Newsletter,* published by the American Friends Service Committee, 2161 Massachusetts Ave., Cambridge, MA 02100, for the article appearing in *Sojourners* as "Crossing Boundaries," but published by the AFSC as "Helping Americans See the Soviets as People."

*Northshore Weeklies, Inc.* September 30, 1984, North Shore, Ipswich, MA 01938, for "From Russia With Love."

*The Other Side,* 300 West Apsley St., Philadelphia, PA 19944, for "Grass-Roots Diplomacy."

*Christianity and Crisis,* Inc., 537 West 121 St., New York, NY 10027, for "In Moscow the Subject Is Peace."

*Mennonite Weekly Review,* Feb. 20, Feb. 27, and March 6, 1986, for "Mennonites Visit Ancestral Homeland."

*Northcoast View,* published by Bearney Publishing Co., Eureka, CA 95502, for "It's Warm in Siberia."

*Fellowship Special Edition* with *International Fellowship of Reconciliation,* published in Nyack, NY 10960, for "To Live Without Enemies."

*The Record,* 150 River St., Hackensack, NJ 07610, for "A Visit to the Soviet Union."

*San Jose Mercury News,* San Jose, CA, for "Soviet Citizens Share Desire for Peace."

Numerous others helped in various ways to develop the manuscript. They include Sanford F. Cutler, Miriam Donohue, Stephen C. Galleher, Sharon Glass, Von Hardesty, Grace Jones, Marcella Kogan, Laurama Pixton, and Nancy Urquhart.

# Contents

Foreword .................................. xi

Introduction ................................ 1

List of Contributors......................... 17

1. Climbers Stage High-Altitude
   Summit Meeting ........................ 19
   *Associated Press Report*

2. Crossing Boundaries .................... 22
   *Andrea Ayvasian*

3. Dancing with Wedding Guests ........... 25
   *John A. Palmer*

4. On Meeting the "Enemy" ................ 27
   *Madeleine Glynn Trichel*

5. The Faces of Olga, Yuri, and Volodya ..... 30
   *Anonymous*

6. From Russia with Love ................... 38
   *Jane Bernhardt*

7. A Glimpse into the Life of a Russian ...... 47
   *Scott Neufeld*

8. God is Still Smiling in Leningrad.......... 50
   *Edith Eckart*

9. Books, Bibles, and Blood Banks .......... 53
   *Clyde E. Weaver*

10. Grass-Roots Diplomacy . . . . . . . . . . . . . . . . . .57
    *Richard Deats*
11. Incident in Leningrad . . . . . . . . . . . . . . . . . . . .66
    *Kent R. Larrabee*
12. In Moscow the Subject is Peace and
    A Letter from Moscow. . . . . . . . . . . . . . . . . . . .70
    *Jim Forest*
13. I was Taken In—a Peace Tour
    to the Soviet Union . . . . . . . . . . . . . . . . . . . . .860
    *Farley W. Wheelwright*
14. Mennonites Visit Ancestral Homeland . . . . .97
    *Paul Schrag*
15. Roots and Wings . . . . . . . . . . . . . . . . . . . . . . .101
    *Danaan Parry*
16. Russian Pictures . . . . . . . . . . . . . . . . . . . . . . .106
    *Winifred Rawlins*
17. Soviet Citizens Share Desire for Peace . . . .117
    *Sharon Tennison*
18. To Live Without Enemies . . . . . . . . . . . . . . . .121
    *Gene Knudsen-Hoffman*
19. Two Faces of Mother Russia . . . . . . . . . . . . .129
    *Jean Lewis-Snable*
20. It's Warm in Siberia . . . . . . . . . . . . . . . . . . . .133
    *Jon Humboldt Gates*
Selected Bibliography . . . . . . . . . . . . . . . . . . . . . .145

# *Foreword*

The essays on the following pages tell an extraordinary story—the awakening of the American people to the human dimensions of life in the Soviet Union. Quietly, almost imperceptibly—and ironically, at a time of harsh rhetoric and reckless arms build-up—a new attitude has been forming in the land. A growing number of people have come to the realization that the United States and the USSR are on a collision course, each the victim of decades of Cold War policies, mutual suspicion, and endless recriminations. Out-moded attitudes and blind stereotypes have magnified our differences beyond all reason and obscured our common humanity and shared destiny on a fragile planet.

Not willing to wait for our leaders to change this dreadful state of affairs, we the people have taken peacemaking into our own hands. By the tens of thousands, Americans have gone to the Soviet Union to meet our supposed enemy face to face. A myriad number of groups and projects have sprung up to signal a new day in US/Soviet relations, from sports to religion, from the arts to education, from politics to ecology. From a handful of relationships to the present multitude, the people have spoken with unmistakable clarity and firmness: we choose life, not death; friendship, not enmity; hope, not despair.

Helen Bailey has brought together a variety of essays that make this story come alive in a fresh and compelling way. We are indebted to her for challenging and inspiring us to further this great drama that is unfolding in our midst.

Richard Deats, Director
US-USSR Reconciliation Project
Fellowship of Reconciliation
Nyack, New York

*YOUNG GIRL*
*Children's Peace Committee,*
*Moscow*

# Introduction

$G$*lasnost,* an openness on the part of the Soviet Union made evident by Communist Party General Secretary Mikhail S. Gorbachev in the fall of 1986, has opened a fresh chapter in East-West relations. Even before this peaceful initiative was felt in the West, it had been gathering momentum on the home front in the Soviet Union. In the United States, however, *glasnost* has brought out a variety of responses, from skepticism about the intent behind the changes being proposed, to an undisguised rejoicing. It is my hope that this proffered friendliness and change from the old "Iron Curtain" days of secrecy means that peace and reconciliation between the superpowers is a genuine possibility.

If the two superpowers can effectively demonstrate an openness toward the other, and if they can end the arms race, the world would surely be a healthier place for all. Such openness would point the way toward a more stable, cooperating world society that accepts *interdependence* as the new way to conserve our planet's resources, our environment, and our peoples. As we seek to understand the Soviet Union, we in the United States may well ask, "Who are the people who live within the confines of this vast multinational state? What are they really like? Would they be called an enemy if we knew them better? By the same token, would they have a more positive attitude toward us if they knew us?"

This book is a first step in finding answers to those questions. It is my belief that we can learn to know the Soviets, generally called "Russians" in the US, as people. In trying to know them it is important to understand from where they have come and what effect their history has had on them. It is also important to interact with them on a people-to-people basis. Indeed as contacts have multiplied with each passing year, many have come to sense that these strangers are our kin in a profound way. They have the same needs and aspirations; they react to love and hate as we do; they fear and trust as we do, and they seek the good in life even as we do. Many Americans and others have seen people in the USSR respond to the visitor's friendly approach with a warm enthusiasm. Russians, after all, are well-known for their hospitality and warmth as well as their historic distrust of foreigners.

The names Tatiana and Ivan are personifications of our sisters and brothers in the USSR as found in the personal experiences and encounters reported here. They are our close relatives in the human race and part of the larger extended global family which, once unknown and unfamiliar, even feared, is now needed in the developing global community. This book is an effort to penetrate the great barriers that history, ideology, geography, and language have created in order to find the human dimension.

The Soviet Union is currently undergoing a renewed effort at modernization and liberalization which affects its relationships with the rest of the world. The Soviet Communist Party's Central Committee describes the reconstruction at home as accelerating the country's socio-economic development. In essence, it involves measures of a revolutionary nature for which they had little choice. Remaining with the status quo was, in fact, a retreat. A new generation of Soviet leaders had to lead their society to qualitatively new levels of development.

The reconstruction, or *perestroika,* is evident in the accelerated process observed in limiting the role of the military in politics. For example, there is no military voice in the powerful Politburo. The war heroes of the past have been succeeded by technically oriented persons. Admiral of the Fleet, Vladimir Chernavin, has stressed cooperation with the other branches of the military. Army Chief-of-Staff, Sergey Akhromeyer, who earned the respect of Americans at the 1986 summit meeting in Reykjavik, along with other military figures, accept Gorbachev's argument that economic and social reforms are the backbone of military strength and the country's security.

Much of what Gorbachev seems to represent, and what the country is embracing, aims at the very heart of the Soviet system. The old Stalinist system of closed doors and central control is not working. Gorbachev, for example, has backed local leaders' demands for greater autonomy and has gone so far as to introduce some market incentives along with a management approach that calls for more decentralization. Evidence indicates again that economic reform is a top priority. Traditionally planned socialist economies—based on Marxist-Leninist models—have been notorious for their top-heavy bureaucracies and non-productivity.

Another evidence of change in the Soviet Union is in the field of communication and the arts. In September 1986 a US-USSR exchange group, "Bridges for Peace," of which I was a part, met with the Soviet Peace Committee in Moscow along with radio and newspaper reporters. We were asked to speak freely into our microphones in answer to the random questions asked by the press. Goodwill was very much in evidence and our American voices were broadcast to the Russian public even as we were about to return home. Our impressions were also recorded in the newspaper *Isvestia.*

Western political leaders were asked to speak on Soviet television in Spring 1987. Prime Minister Margaret Thatcher spoke bluntly about what was needed in the Soviet Union to make negotiations between the East and West successful. Secretary of State George Schultz openly criticized Soviet policies with special reference to human rights, underscoring his words with attendance at a synagogue service. The release of some political prisoners, including Andrei Sakharov, is also a hopeful sign.

Artists sense that the new *glasnost* may have begun a renaissance in Soviet culture, and change in artistic and intellectual fields is taking place more rapidly than in the economic and political areas. Americans need to be aware, however, that in periods of liberalization the Soviets typically extend greater freedom to the arts. Once the top leadership goes after the economy and the military, it is more certain that radical reforms are underway. Khrushchev, for example, was toppled in October 1964 for trying to refashion the latter. A kind of revolution has also taken place among Soviet women, who traditionally have been overburdened and undervalued in fields that men have claimed as their own. Women are now expressing feminism and even anger in their need for recognition.

Today more people in the USSR read the newspapers; circulation was up by fourteen million in the winter and spring months of 1987. Television presentations of rock music concerts, formerly viewed as a decadent development of the western world, are shown. Current women's fashions from abroad are shown and inspire domestic creation. These changes represent a profound desire for freedom among a wide spectrum of people. An important source of Gorbachev's support is the widespread realization that more freedom of expression was imperative. The needs of the people had to be met.

Perhaps the greatest desire of all, however, as affirmed again and again in the experiences reported in this book, is the people's desire for peace. They who have suffered so much from war have a passionate desire for peace, and for the common security against the threat of nuclear weapons that could lead to war. This concern is heard everywhere. The genuine desire for peace has been shaped by historical events and, unlike party propaganda and policies, is deeply integrated in the consciousness of the people.

The reforms both within the Soviet Union and in outward relations with other countries seem to have been fueled by socio-economic needs and from the artists and writers straining for creative freedom. The underlying motives for *glasnost,* however, are extremely complex. Boris Pasternak in *Dr. Zhivago* (to be published in the Soviet Union for the first time in 1988) said in a typically Russian image, "The first signs of spring—thaw—the air smells of buttered pancakes and vodka, as at Shrovetide."

Refreshing signs of spring are becoming evident in the film industry with the relaxation of strict censorship. Gleb Panfilov, an innovative film director who had submitted *Tema (The Theme)* for approval in 1979, was turned down until *glasnost* opened the way. His productions won over *Platoon* in the International Film Festival in West Berlin in March 1987. The theme of his film was about artistic compromise, expressed in sensitive terms surrounding Jewish emigration. Now Yelm Klimov, a newly appointed director of a commission that has begun releasing previously censored movies and investigating injustices in the film industry, is moving ahead with creative productions.

In a union of fifteen republics, whose combined population is two hundred and eighty million people, religion has persisted as a powerful force, despite the official atheism of the USSR. Historically, the Russian Orthodox Church was the religion of the majority of the population, the central focus of Russian nationality, and until 1917, closely tied to the Russian imperial state. Religion, however, has not died out; it has flourished even under suppression. Three seminaries of the Russian Orthodox Church and a few monasteries—whose property like that of all Russian Orthodox churches still belongs to the state—have weathered the storm. The Trinity monastery at Zagorsk, founded in 1337, was once the rallying point for Russian national salvation during invasions. Today, it is a shrine for St. Sergius, a beloved Russian saint. At one time, it was the home of Rublev's famed icon of the Trinity. Since 1946 religious life has been permitted there and Zagorsk has resumed its role as the spiritual center of all Russia. It has become a place of pilgrimage for believer and tourist alike. People press into operating Orthodox churches, standing as is their custom shoulder to shoulder, filling the beautiful edifices with song and fervent piety. In 1988, the 1000-year anniversary of the coming of Christianity to Russia (at Kiev) will be observed with numerous celebrations. Under *glasnost,* the Russian Orthodox Church has been given back the Danilovsky monastery which will be the new home of the Moscow Patriarch.

The poet, Yevgeni Yevtushenko, wrote in 1963:

> *I am a daughter of Russia,*
> *a land you cannot understand.*
> *From its childhood*
> *this land was christened with the lash,*
> *torn to shreds,*
> *burned.*
> *Its soul was trampled underfoot.*
> *It was dealt blow after blow,*
> *by the Pechenegs,*
> *Varangians,*
> *Tartars,*
> *and by its own people—*
> *even worse than the Tartars.*

These few lines convey the inheritance of these early scattered and tormented people. The Russians were an easy mark for invading Mongolian tribes from the East, and while they were still small farmers and fur traders gathered in scattered towns and villages under local princes, they were invaded from the north and west by the Swedes, Lithuanians, Poles, and in more modern times by the French and Germans.

The history of Russia is fascinating. It seems obvious that a passionate love of their land, a certain distrust of foreigners, and a submission to authority have been characteristics of the peoples who settled in this region. The political origins of the Russian state date from the ninth century, although eastern Slavic peoples had settled along the Dnieper River and her tributaries much earlier. The ancient cities of Kiev, Novgorod, and Vladimir formed economic centers controlled by Norsemen whose trading routes led to Byzantium.

In A.D. 988, Prince Vladimir of Kiev decided that a state religion could foster political unity. He chose Eastern Orthodoxy as experienced by his emissaries in Byzantium because of its splendor and beauty. The Russian language which was adapted to the Greek alphabet by the Byzantine missionary, St. Cyril, later made possible the birth of Russian literature. Byzantine art and architecture were also adopted. When the Catholic and Orthodox Churches divided in 1054, Russian Christianity was isolated from the Catholic Church in central and western Europe. The Byzantine influence was so thorough, that after the fall of Constantinople in 1453, Moscow (founded in the 12th century) was regarded as the "third Rome."

Between 1240 and 1480 the Kievan state was battered time after time by waves of invaders. Genghis Khan overran Russia from the east. German and Swedish forces attacked from the north. This period was dominated by the Tartars, the "Golden Horde," who conquered much of Asia and some of eastern Europe. The people were forced to pay tribute to their conquerors, but they were held together by the spirituality of the Orthodox Church.

During the 1460s and 70s the Grand Duke of Moscow, Ivan III, united the area encompassing Novgorad, Kiev, and Moscow. He forced the withdrawal of the Tartars and designated himself Tzar (Caesar). Although he provided the state with a central administration, his rule began a long tradition of autocratic monarchs. Ivan IV, the Terrible, further solidified the young Muscovite state but in his later years ruled by terror, and eventually went mad. This was followed by the "Time of Troubles" (1598–1613) which began when Boris Godunov, brother-in-law of Ivan IV, occupied the throne. Poland and Sweden invaded. Cossacks in the Ukraine rebelled. Near chaos reigned in Moscow as two pretenders sought the crown. Finally, an assembly of Russian Boyars, wealthy merchants who became the aristocracy, sought a Tzar who would rally the people behind him and preserve Russian independence. In 1613 Prince Mikhail Romanov was selected. He fought off the Poles and stabilized the government, thus beginning the Romanov dynasty that lasted for three centuries, up until the Revolution in 1917.

One of the better known figures of the long and arduous struggle to become a modern nation was Peter I (the Great), 1682–1725, the Tzar who wanted trade with the West, education for his people, and European culture for his country. He knew that trade required a foothold on the Baltic Sea and a navy to support it. He helped to build the ships and imported foreign craftsmen to teach the necessary skills to his subjects. Peter encouraged the founding of factories, schools, the study of medicine, publishing, a newspaper, and the theater in Moscow. He built the new capital of St. Petersburg (1703) on the Neva River. He modernized the army and fought off Swedish invasions, defeating them at the battle of Poltava, 1709.

Peter's modernization program brought wealth and position to the gentry, as well as subordination for the peasantry and the clergy. He brought the Orthodox Church more firmly under state control, and he also reorganized the civil service. Although Peter's behavior was sometimes barbaric, his accomplishments were of tremendous significance for Russia. His reign brought a deliberate effort to superimpose Western reforms from the top down which also brought division.

A subsequent ruler of great power and influence was Catherine the Great, the German wife of the nephew of Elizabeth, Peter's daughter, who ruled from 1762 to 1796. She was intelligent and governed with an iron will. Catherine craved power, extravagant jewels, and palaces. She dallied with the ideas embodied in the European Enlightenment, a philosophy that influenced the framers of our own constitution. A peasant uprising at that time, however, led by Cossacks put an end to its fulfillment in Russia. Catherine successfully ended a long war with Turkey and extended Russian borders in the south and west.

Some people have thought that Russia lost an opportunity to reform the nation through enlightened ideas of "freedom" and "equality" during Catherine's reign. While the Russian court was increasingly patterned after the "enlightened despots" of eighteenth century Europe, the tragic results of autocratic rule were everywhere. Russia was enfeebled by a greed for power and self-indulgence, impoverished by extravagances, and left with an aggrieved peasantry.

The next century witnessed the French invasion by Napoleon Bonaparte (1812), who was turned back primarily because of a terrible winter at Moscow. The Decembrist Revolt in 1825, led by army officers, was a demonstration in St. Petersburg for dynastic change. They wanted an abolition of serfdom and the creation of a constitutional monarchy, not Tzarist absolutism. They were imbued with the democratic ideals of the French Revolution. The revolt failed and the leaders were hanged. The serfs were finally freed in 1861.

In 1905 Russia lost a war with Japan, a humiliating defeat because her fleet was destroyed by that tiny island nation. At this time, thousands of workers seeking economic and social reforms and their families gathered at the Winter Palace where they expected to place their grievances before Tzar Nicholas II. Palace guards opened fire on the crowd killing 500 men, women, and children. This "Bloody Sunday" enraged the populace. Nicholas, a mild man, tried too late to grant their demand for an elected assembly *(Duma)*.

The outbreak of World War I in 1914 caught the Romanov regime unprepared. The army was not equipped to enter a war against the Germans and the Russian army retreated with heavy casualties. The social fabric of the nation could not grapple with the demands of a prolonged and brutal war.

The early 1917 revolution broke out. Mobs of striking workers and soldiers in mutiny set fires to police stations and opened the jails releasing the prisoners. Political action committees were formed by soldiers. The Tzar resigned, ending a thousand years of monarchy in Russia.

There was an attempt to set up a democratic provisional government but factions of intellectuals, land owners, peasants, and radicals could not hold it together. That same year a new factor was added: Vladimir Lenin returned from seventeen years of study and plotting revolution with the Marxists in Europe. He and Bolshevik revolutionaries occupied government offices in St. Petersburg in November 1917.

Russia left the European war, but the "imperialist war" was soon changed into a civil one. The Red Army fought against the White Army, which had some popular support as well as aid from the forces of fourteen foreign countries, including the United States. The fighting lasted until 1920 and cost the lives of five million people, including the Tzar and his family. The Union of Soviet Socialist Republics emerged as the world's first communist state.

After Lenin died in 1924, power was concentrated in the hands of Josef Stalin, who ruthlessly set about eliminating his rivals and transforming Russia. He forced agriculture and state farms at a terrible price in human suffering. He undertook the "Great Purge" to destroy any opposition, real and imagined. Some estimate that twenty million people were sent to work camps or killed as a result of Stalin's policies.

Just prior to the outbreak of World War II, in 1939, Stalin made a nonaggression pact with Hitler whereby they would carve up Poland in the event of war. If Stalin hoped to avoid fighting with Germany, his plan failed. In 1941 Hitler marched the *wehrmacht* into Russia, but was defeated eventually at great cost to the Soviet people. (20,000,000 lives were lost amid great suffering.)

After the war, Stalin was quick to set up a barrier of states friendly to the Soviet Union in eastern Europe. These formed an "Iron Curtain" to insure that Russia would not be invaded from Europe again. Stalin, and later Nikita Khrushchev and Leonid Breshnev laid claim to world power status in military might, industrial development, and advances in science and culture. Beginning in 1957, the powerful image and cruel programs of Stalin were repudiated. A period of détente with the West began in the 1970s.

Today as a superpower competing with the United States in a world power struggle for dominance through the production of ever more devastating nuclear weapons, the Soviet Union has shown an eagerness for dialogue. Indeed, both nations have sought to build links for stability and understanding even as they both have engaged in an arms race.

In confrontation, nations use propaganda, but people, singly and in groups, who are determined to find the truth are meeting, sharing their fears of war and their hopes for peace. One such group has been the International Physicians for Social Reponsibility, inspired by the combined efforts of physicians both in the Soviet Union and in the United States, notably Dr. Eugene Chazov, physician to the Kremlin, and Dr. Bernard Lown, Harvard School of Public Health. This group has spoken to tens of millions of people through newspapers, television talk shows, and international telecasts, warning all peoples against the use of nuclear weapons and modern warfare. They have bridged the boundaries between nations and ideologies to affirm with President Dwight D. Eisenhower: "The true security problem . . . is not merely man against man, or nation against nation. It is man against war." Albert Einstein warned us: "We shall require a substantially new manner of thinking if we are to survive."

In the meantime, activities of cooperation between the US and USSR have included an astronaut link-up in outer space, preservation of wildlife habitats, scientific and medical research, artistic and cultural exchanges of all kinds and, perhaps most important, exchange visits of people on goodwill tours.

---

The following essays, written by Americans returning home after a visit to the Soviet Union, reveal a common thread that many did not expect to find. Each traveler found that these people who had been labeled "the enemy" were very much like themselves. These strangers suffered pain, loved their children, and were desperately pleading for a peace that would ensure all children a chance to live out their lives without the fear of war. The Americans saw that the Soviets were part and parcel of the created order to which they also belonged and they found a deep satisfaction in this discovery. They want to share their experiences that tell of kindred spirits who have the same needs and aspirations as they know in themselves.

"Climbers Stage High-Altitude Summit Meeting" is a news wire service story about mountain climbers William Garner and Randy Starrett. Their achievement with a team of Soviet climbers received national attention before the November Summit Meeting between President Reagan and Soviet leader Gorbachev in 1985 at Geneva, Switzerland. This was surely an exhilarating experience even for seasoned mountain climbers, but doubly so as they could sense that the world's problems would approach solution if the leaders met, not in man-made conference halls, but in the mountains where the world without boundaries could be seen and experienced.

"Crossing Boundaries" by Andrea Ayvazian was an experience that the author expected to be an intellectual exercise on a fact-finding trip to the Soviet Union. Instead, she found it to be a journey of the heart. Others on the same Volga River Peace Cruise have related that she gave so much of herself that she stimulated the whole group and those they met in affectionate response. She found paradoxes in the Soviet economy, the superpower where many tradespeople still use the abacus, and where shoppers wait patiently in long lines for limited supplies. Andrea found only friendship wherever the group went.

Two short accounts of insightful incidents follow. In each case the experience reveals a common humanity which converted the writer from "show me" to "let me tell you what I discovered." These accounts are: "Dancing with Wedding Guests" by John A. Palmer and "On Meeting the 'Enemy' " by Madeleine Glynn Trichel.

In the anonymous essay, "The Faces of Olga, Yuri, and Volodya," the author shares experiences about participation in the religious life of the Russian Orthodox Church. It is a captivating description of the power and simplicity of a faith that shuns personal pride, worldly success, and seeks to offer self as a ransom for others in need. In contrast to the mysterious beauty of icons, church architecture, and liturgy, the believer's life is shown as self-effacing, obedient, and humble.

"From Russia with Love" is the record of a young mother, Jane Bernhardt, who went as an artist to learn about the people of the Soviet Union first hand. She had an opportunity to meet with young workers on the streets with her sketch pad in hand and she was introduced to the history of the land through the kindred spirit of another young artist in Moscow. Jane shared her differences with the Soviets. She loved them and was shocked by the lack of understanding and a tirade of propaganda from members of the American press.

"A Glimpse into the Life of a Russian" by Scott Neufeld describes a visit to the apartment of a young Leningrad plumber. "God is Still Smiling in Leningrad" by Edith Eckart, is a description of attendance at a Baptist church while in that city. Clyde E. Weaver, a veteran book marketer, gives his impression of the Moscow International Book Fair in "Books, Bibles, and Blood Banks." All of these American visitors were overjoyed at the warm receptions and gestures of friendship they received.

"Grass Roots Diplomacy: Reconciling the Superpowers" by Richard Deats is an example of the reconciling work carried on by the Fellowship of Reconciliation. Because of the FOR's reputation as a nonpartisan group reaching out into trouble spots with friendship and understanding, this pacifist organization has been able to promote high standards of peace and justice not only with individuals but with high ranking officials and organizations in numerous countries.

The contribution of Kent R. Larrabee, "Incident in Leningrad," shows a Quaker's pilgrimage to find the "light" in a people hidden for so long from us. His witness was a very direct and personal approach to peacemaking.

Jim Forest's essay, "In Moscow the Subject is Peace," describes his visits to and impressions of the official Soviet Peace Committee and the independent Group for Trust between the US and the USSR. How genuine is their desire for peace? He learned much about the people of the country through these interviews—their commitments and loyalty to their country—with a few surprises. In a recent letter, this author reports on the great Peace Forum, called together by invitation from Mikhail Gorbachev, of a thousand people from around the world and held in Moscow in February 1987.

"I Was Taken In," written by Farley W. Wheelwright, retired Unitarian Universalist minister, contrasts a 1983 tour with a visit to the USSR in 1954. Although his perceptions are sometimes quite different from other writers in this collection, he admits to being "taken in" by full employment, free health care, efforts at housing, the priority of children, and the work of the Soviet Peace Committee.

"Mennonites Visit Ancestral Homeland in Soviet Union" by Paul Schrag is a shortened version of a longer account of a college tour to former Mennonite villages in the Ukraine. Sponsored by two Mennonite colleges in Kansas, the study group included many who are descendants of Russian émigrés of the 1870s. They were particularly pleased to be able to worship with a Mennonite Brethren congregation in the remote Kirgiz Socialist Republic.

Danaan Parry, who wrote "Roots and Wings," is the founder and director of Holyearth Foundation, an organization that maintains the Earthstewards Network with goodwill missions to the Soviet Union and the sponsorship of Soviet visits to the United States. Parry's article reveals an American's growing understanding of people whom he feared before discovering them. He senses the uniqueness of the Russians, their passionate nature, their group unconsciousness, their fervent love of their land. He offers them wings. At this writing, some have found wings, as others will, to risk creative self-expression.

"Russian Pictures" is a long, narrative poem, only portions of which are reprinted here, by Winifred Rawlins. Through Quaker eyes, she has captured expressions of the robust Russian character in the complex mystery of common life. There are images of voices of the mixed comraderie on a summer weekend, prayers at Zagorsk, a visit to Tchaikovsky's home and the piano at which he composed, and even a visit to the circus.

"US and USSR Citizens Share Desire for Peace" by Sharon Tennison recounts the freedom of movement this group of fifteen from California experienced as they traveled around Moscow. They had the good fortune to have had a camera crew with them so that when the group stayed together everything could be recorded.

"To Live Without Enemies" by Gene Knudsen-Hoffman comes from contact made the previous year with a woman in the Soviet Union. Gene was asked to bring together Russian religious women and American religious women in the United States in a setting where they could learn to know each other better. The meeting was held in Santa Barbara, California with four Soviet women and American women from across the country representing various denominations. In this unique experience the participants learned what it meant "to love the stranger."

In the short piece by Jean Lewis-Snable, "Two Faces of Mother Russia," the author, a mother herself, senses a close identity with the symbols of Mother Russia. Two statues at the war memorial at Volgograd suggest the mother who urges her children onward to victory and the mother who weeps over the sacrifice. This is a sensitive and subjective response to an encounter with the soul of a people so frequently torn by war.

Finally, "It's Warm in Siberia" by Jon Humboldt Gates was taken from the author's daily journal while on a visit to the Soviet Union. The scene of his encounter with a student at Lake Baikal in Siberia is near the Mongolian border in a mountainous region. Anton's eagerness to welcome the stranger and take him home to his parents was irresistible, and Jon agrees to accept this warmth and generosity on the part of the peasant family—to his own enjoyment and an understanding of friendship across the boundaries of nations and language.

*Helen Bailey is founder and president of the International Peace Museum in Washington, DC. In 1984, after visiting the Soviet Union, she developed a Resource Center for Nonviolence in Morristown, NJ. An active Episcopalian, Mrs. Bailey served on the National Council of the Fellowship of Reconciliation, 1982–1983, and has been active in World Peacemakers and other peace organizations.*

# List of Contributors

Andrea Ayvasian, Director of the Peace Development
   Fund, Amherst, MA
John A. Palmer, businessman, Morristown, NJ
Madeleine Glynn Trichel, Director of the Center for Peace
   at St. Stephen's Episcopal Church, Columbus, OH
Anonymous, a literary scholar involved in ecumenical
   study of Roman Catholic-Eastern Orthodox relations
Jane Bernhardt, freelance artist, Beverly, MA
Scott Neufeld, student, Bethel College, North Newton,
   KS
Edith Eckart, Center for Creative Peacemaking, Arcata,
   CA
Clyde E. Weaver, New Call to Peacemaking, Elgin, IL
Richard Deats, Director of Interfaith Activities, Fellow-
   ship of Reconciliation, Nyack, NY
Kent R. Larrabee, psychotherapist, Philadelphia, PA
Jim Forest, General Secretary of the International
   Fellowship of Reconciliation, Alkmaar, Holland
Farley W. Wheelwright, retired Unitarian Universalist
   minister, Sherman Oaks, CA
Paul Schrag, staff writer for the *Mennonite Weekly Review,*
   North Newton, KS
Danaan Parry, Director of the Holyearth Foundation,
   Bainbridge Island, WA
Winifred Rawlins, poet, Moylan, PA
Sharon Tennison, Registered Nurse, Cupertino, CA

Gene Knudson-Hoffman, writer and peace advocate, Santa Barbara, CA

Jean Lewis-Snable, retired public school teacher, Basking Ridge, NJ

Jon Humboldt Gates, author, Trinidad, CA

# Climbers Stage High-Altitude Summit Meeting
## (Associated Press)

William Garner and Randy Starrett, back from their own summit with the Soviets, may have a useful lesson for Ronald Reagan and Mikhail Gorbachev, one they learned on the windswept peak of a 24,406-foot mountain in Soviet Central Asia last summer.

It is the same message the two young Washington area residents left atop Pik Pobedy—"Victory Peak"—the Soviet Union's second-highest mountain, which they conquered August 22, 1985, along with an American movie cameraman, David Breashears, and a dozen of the Soviet Union's most skillful alpine climbers.

On a piece of paper, sealed in plastic and left inside a World War II Soviet artillery shell casing hauled to the summit, the two Americans wrote in English and Russian:

"We, the American team on the first joint Soviet-American expedition up Pik Pobedy, have climbed this mountain to illustrate for the people of our two countries how much greater value there is in our learning to take risks together, than in our continuing to put the world at risk through mutual confrontation."

Perhaps mindful of the scheduled November 19–20 summit meeting between President Reagan and Soviet leader Gorbachev in Geneva, Switzerland, the Soviet climbing leader put it another way during a celebratory exchange of vodka and champagne toasts on their return from the peak.

As Starrett recalls, one of his Soviet comrades said that "if the world's leaders were alpinists and could come together in the mountains, the world's problems would vanish."

The harrowing, nine-day climb made Soviet heroes of Garner, 36, an independent consultant and Soviet affairs analyst here, and Starrett, 43, a trial lawyer from suburban Fairfax County, Virginia.

The two have been climbing mountains together for 15 years, in North and South America and in Europe, but they are the first foreigners to ascend Pik Pobedy, which lies on the Soviet border with China in the Tien Shan mountain range.

It is the world's northernmost peak above 7,000 meters or 23,100 feet, well into the so-called "death zone" where climbers must use oxygen or risk a speedy death. Pobedy is so treacherous that it has claimed more lives— in excess of 60—than all the attempts on Mount Everest, the world's highest at 29,028 feet.

"It was one of the toughest climbs of my life," a smiling Garner, sun-tanned and frost-bitten, said at the conclusion of the climb, when the expedition was hailed as commemorating the Allied victory in World War II, 40 years ago.

With that triumph, Garner and Starrett also became the first foreigners to receive the coveted "Order of the Snow Leopard" for climbing all four of the Soviet Union's peaks higher than 23,000 feet.

They had climbed 24,590 foot Pik Kommunizma in the Pamirs mountains in 1982, viewing both China and Afghanistan from its summit, and returned to the Pamirs last year to scale both Pik Korzhenevskaya, 23,305 feet, and Pik Lenin, 23,400 feet, in just three weeks.

It took 10 months for Garner, with help from the host Soviet Sports Committee, to win the Kremlin's permission for the joint expedition to climb Pik Pobedy, which no American had ever attempted before.

Once on the slopes, braving 80 mph gusts that whipped them with blinding snow and ice, the two Americans developed a kinship with, and a new respect for, their Soviet companions.

# Crossing Boundaries

## *Andrea Ayvazian*

It has been difficult and sometimes impossible to discuss in a casual fashion my three-and-a-half-week journey to the Soviet Union. It was a compact and concentrated time—the intensity left me reeling. I find I am still sifting through and sorting out memories of my Soviet experiences to understand their meaning and deal with my emotional response. Many months have passed, and I still feel as though I had eaten a large, rich meal that hasn't digested.

Two themes emerge from the journey: it was an experience of paradox and surprise. Before leaving, I considered myself a sophisticated traveler; informed, prepared, and highly educated about the Soviet Union. I regarded the trip as a fact-finding mission; after years of working on issues of peace and disarmament, I was finally traveling to the Soviet Union.

I intended to probe the hard issues and to press for answers to the questions so often put before me. I packed three large empty notebooks and a ridiculous assortment of pens. I regarded the trip as a journey that would be predominantly an intellectual experience, rather like the way I visit museums—studying each scene with care and then moving on.

The trip was not at all what I expected. Yes, I discussed sensitive issues and asked hard questions. But far more than an intellectual experience, it was a journey of the heart. I did not fill the three notebooks I had so carefully packed, but almost daily, I played my guitar and sang with newly-made Soviet friends. (My guitar—that cumbersome addition I decided at the last moment to take along!)

How unexpected that "the enemy" would greet us with arms outspread, offer us bouquets of roses, buy us rounds of vodka, toast our children and theirs, and dance until the sun rose over the Volga River. Imagine my surprise when Soviets repeatedly invited us into their homes, served us caviar on bakery bread, stuffed gifts into my purse, and said with feeling: "Come back again, and stay longer." They related to me as an individual, as *I related to them.* There was a mutual unspoken understanding that each of us was not to be confused with our respective governments' administration.

The experience was also one of deep paradox; things were not always as they seemed. The greatest paradox and contrast was the gap between the USSR as "the other great world power" and the standard of living of most Soviet citizens. This is the nation that can produce and deploy sophisticated SS-20 missiles, the same country in which it is nearly impossible to buy a hairbrush. This nation can match the United States with advanced military technology, but department store clerks total shoppers' bills with an abacus.

I expected to visit "the other superpower." Instead I found a country that felt far more like the Third World nations I have traveled through. During the entire stay, I kept thinking about the expression so popular in the US peace movement today: "You can't have both guns and butter." The Soviets certainly do have guns, and they certainly do not have butter. Their diet is limited; potatoes, bread, and cabbage are staples. Paper products are hard to find; envelopes are a rare commodity and facial tissues are nonexistent.

This superpower is a poor nation with a struggling economy. The technology created for its advanced weapons systems has not even begun to trickle down to everyday life. Museums in the Tartar Republic exhibit shower heads in the display cases, a proud indicator of modern inventions.

I found a nation in lock-step competition to keep up in the arms race and eager to present Americans as the aggressive enemy. But I also found Soviet people who look to the West with a mixture of envy and awe. Our clothing, our heroes, even our subway chatter fascinated them.

After spending three days exploring Yerevan, in Armenia, with a newly-made Soviet friend, I said to him upon leaving: "Levon, what can I send you from the US? Books, poetry, tapes?" After thinking for a long time, Levon finally said in his perfect English: "There is nothing you can send me. You are a window on the West. Just return and talk to me for another three days."

Since coming home I have shown my slides and talked about the Soviet Union at numerous engagements. American audiences—whether they are church groups, the Kiwanis Club, university students, or peace organizations—respond to the slides of Soviet people. The beautiful architecture and pastoral scenes interest them less than the blurry shots of Soviet families boating in Gorky Park, old women selling roses on street corners, babies in prams, and lovers in the park. Soviet faces move American people.

Propaganda abounds in both countries. There are myths and stereotypes, untruths and fears. And yet, after seeing 121 slides of Soviet citizens at work at construction sites, in line for apples, performing Siberian dances, and singing alongside Americans, people seemed to come away with a different feeling.

I remember the question posed by Wendell Berry in his poem "To a Siberian Woodsman":

> *Who has imagined your death negligible*
> *    to me*
> *now that I have seen these pictures of*
> *    your face?*

# Dancing with Wedding Guests

## *John Palmer*

One of the most vivid impressions I have from my two weeks as a tourist in Russia last fall [1985] was the contact we had with a wedding party in a restaurant outside Kiev, in the Ukraine.

Our party of tourists occupied about half the dining room while the other half was occupied by a bride and groom, their friends and relatives. They had just been married. There was an orchestra at one end of the dining room playing what were evidently the latest Soviet dance tunes. The music was loud and fast.

My wife, a grandmother herself, decided that she wanted to meet the *Babushkas* (Russian grandmothers) in the wedding party. Our interpreter obliged and my wife was given a very friendly reception when introduced as an American grandmother. The *Babushkas* couldn't have been more pleased and friendly, and through the interpreter they had a wonderful visit. During this time I was sitting alone at the table when the mother of the groom came over and practically dragged me to the dance floor. We had a terrific time! Russians dance to very loud music with stamping and some shouting.

Nothing would do but we must toast them and they us with homemade vodka prepared for the occasion by the groom's family. Toward the end of the evening, the bride gave her bridal bouquet to our tour group leader.

This was a most unusual gesture, since a bride is expected to leave her bouquet at an unknown soldier's monument, on Lenin's tomb, or at another national monument.

This heart-warming occasion symbolizes to me that the ordinary citizens of Russia, as well as those of other countries, really wish to be friendly with each other and that if we could meet and know each other better, we could all be friends. The arms race with its political leaders and overtones of terror could then be forgotten and we would find the world a better place in which to live.

# 4

# On Meeting the "Enemy"

## *Madeleine Glynn Trichel*

From the Christian communities in Moscow, Zagorsk, Volgograd, Tashkent, and Leningrad, I bring greetings. Your brothers and sisters in Christ send you their tears and prayers, their smiles and their hopes for peace. I am back safe and sound, with more stories than you want to hear. I will be telling stories about this journey for a long time, because it has changed me in ways I can only begin to see.

You've already heard the bad news from the Soviet Union. The Church persecuted. Believers must practice their religion under very difficult circumstances. Leaders of unregistered churches are imprisoned. Human rights are often violated. Jews are particularly oppressed. There are too many government restrictions and too few working churches. All of this is true. Some of it I have seen with my own eyes.

There is good news, too. The Church in the Soviet Union is very much alive. There are millions of believers. Often they must travel long distances from home to attend worship services, but they crowd the churches. Churches were full even at times when American visitors were not expected.

Believers welcomed us with tears and hugs, candy and flowers, prayers and speeches, with pealing bells and music. They kissed me, talked to me, told me the names of those they had lost in war. They told me they are afraid and said they don't want to die. They wished me the clear skies of peace.

We learned that Soviet believers pray for us. Some of them think we have a harder time than they do. They told me: "We know where our struggle lies, we know the cost of being faithful; it is easier for us. You in the West have to struggle with the materialism of your culture, and that is much more difficult." They pray for us.

Already our journey has made a difference. Before we arrived, the Soviets were calling us "The Peace Invasion." Many in our delegation were told privately that our visit had already made things easier for the Church. People everywhere were astonished by our presence and our numbers.

As for meeting the enemy, I kept remembering . . . the Episcopal Church General Convention's document *To Make Peace.* In the section on loving the enemy, we are encouraged to live the Gospel by seeing enemies as individuals, and to be sure to do good to enemies as if to friends.

On an airplane from Moscow to Volgograd—sitting next to a Soviet military officer—I realized he was "my enemy" for sure. He offered me chewing gum. I asked if he spoke English; no, only Russian. He gave me a soft drink. I got out pictures of my kids. He asked if I spoke German. No, did he speak French or Spanish? No. So I got out a Russian phrase book and handed it to my enemy. He read the whole thing and loved it. And then he taught me the Russian alphabet, and we asked each other questions by pointing to phrases in the book. We sat there, shoulder to shoulder, heads bent over our little book, my enemy and I. He wouldn't tell me his name, and I kept wondering if he was one who might send bombs to Columbus.

Before we landed, I gave him my peace button. He said he couldn't wear it on his uniform. I said, "I know. Put it in your pocket." He said, "Here?" and he put it in his coat pocket.

That encounter is another sign of the grace I felt over our journey. I was given the gift of seeing my enemy as an individual. As for him—he knows one of his enemies by name, he has seen pictures of our family and Christmas tree; he has looked into her face.

*MIKHAIL*
*Poet,*
*Leningrad*

5

# The Faces of Olga, Yuri, and Volodya

## *Anonymous*

Like most Russian believers, I am an Orthodox Christian. Though a US citizen, I have work that takes me to Russia for about a month at a time. I speak Russian. Thus in Moscow and Leningrad, Kiev and Kishinev, Odessa and Kazan, I have passed as a Russian Christian, taken the sacraments in their churches, and shared regular fellowship with believers.

I have never been a part of any official religious delegation. My friendships are with lay people in the Orthodox Church, whom I see unescorted. I know a few Catholics in Leningrad and the Baltic republics, but I have never met any of the Baptist or evangelical minority. Despite sporadic media attention to the problems of Christianity in Russia, I am troubled that Americans know so little of Russian Christians. It is not right that our brothers and sisters in the Soviet Union should be faceless. They deserve to have us see, briefly, a small slice of their spirit.

The church is everywhere in the Soviet Union. Let me assure you that Christianity, especially in its Orthodox form, is pervasive in Russia. Many Russians identify themselves quite frankly as "believers," a term much more frequent than "Christian." They pray. If a working church is within commuting distance, they worship openly. If there is no church close by, they go to the great trouble to find one.

Westerners can be blind to the Spirit in Russia because they do not recognize its Orthodox form. Believers and nonbelievers are not quite so incessantly polarized as we might suspect. The Russian grandmother babysitting in the park is likely to be a Christian and to teach her grandchildren the sign of the cross and basic prayers before they ever learn the official atheist line. Families often split along theological lines—a brother is a believer, an aunt belongs to the Party, a grandmother is piously observant (all too many of the grandfathers died in the war), yet a daughter is ignorant of religious matters but believes, somehow, in a God.

Lenin is as omnipresent an image in Russia as are the well-fed, dazzle-smiled models who symbolize the good life in US advertising. Any of these images can stand in the way of the gospel, but none of them can kill it. Our Christian social movement in the United States has been shaped in reaction to the consumer culture. Under socialism, surrounded by idealized images of the worker, burdened by antireligious legislation, the Spirit in Russia has taken on its own subtle shades that can instruct us as we discern them.

Clearly, the ministry of the church in Russia is very different from our own, at least in its emphasis. Christians take contradiction totally for granted. Pecherskaya Lavra, the Monastery of the Caves in Kiev famous among Orthodox as the cradle of Russian Christendom, is now a museum complex. At the entrance to the caverns where the hallowed monks are buried, guides assemble the groups they will lead through the caves.

I watched a Russian group from Leningrad. They nodded agreeably as the guide recited, in a bored monotone, the "superstitions" of the monks and the supposed miracle which preserved the bodies in the dry, natural embalming which the caves provided. Some even took notes.

Out of curiosity, and with some Orthodox outrage at the tone of the guide and the simplistic antireligious slogans on the walls, I tagged onto the end of the single-file procession through the narrow, twisting caves. I was not prepared for what I saw. The guide, far ahead, was well out of sight. The Russians at the end of the line crossed themselves. Many bowed, as is our custom, before the relics. Some left petitions for prayer scratched on shreds of paper, stuffing them into the icon-studded niches in the walls. And these were the same people who nodded so agreeably to the guide. Their resistance takes a different form, you see, from our own.

Christians in Russia begin by taking the last place at the banquet. Western visitors to Russia often conclude that the churches are filled with the old and uneducated. Seldom do they discover, unless they worship and converse with believers, that Christians dress like and have the demeanor of the old and the rejected. Believers in Russia "dress down" for church, in direct contradiction of our own custom.

Christianity in Russia is incompatible with success. Those who desire the Soviet equivalent of rising the corporate ladder can hardly speed that rise with membership at the right parish. To become a regular worshiper is to choose the way of Christ over the way of the world. As the psalm goes, chanted at the beginning of every Orthodox liturgy in Russia, "Put not your trust in princes, in sons of men, in whom there is no salvation" (Psalm 146:3).

Following that psalm, the Russian choir intones the beatitudes, which draw the congregation into their spell. They are the laws of the kingdom proclaimed in the liturgy, and they embody the spirituality of the Russian church. It is hard to convey the joyous spirit, the almost palpable faith at the monastery in Zagorsk as the masses of pilgrims join the choir in singing, "Blessed are you when men shall revile you, and persecute you, and say all manner of evil against you falsely, for my sake, for great is your reward in heaven."

I feel God's presence nowhere so strongly as I do in Russia. The Soviet posters proclaim the worker triumphant over the material conditions of his being. The Soviet church has incorporated some of the same consciousness and, in the grand ideological transformation (or subversion) typical of our faith, the church has transfigured it. Christ the worker, Christ the peasant, Christ the fool triumphs over the powerful, the rich, and the wise.

Christians in Russia focus upon the self-emptying of God, the divine condescension of Christ in becoming human, as their spiritual model. Mary, the *Bogoroditsa,* "Birth-giver of God," is a manifestation of God immanent in the humble.

Yuri is a solemn young engineering student in Leningrad. He scowls when he walks, as do many Russians—you've met these faces in our media portraits of Soviets. Daily, you will find him with the same round, Slavic face rapt in prayer before an icon of the Mother of God in one of Leningrad's churches.

Yuri had only a copy of the Gospels, not in modern Russian but in the liturgical language of Old Church Slavonic, which he studied to better understand the Word. Given a Bible as a gift, he scanned the modern Russian text through tears of gratitude. (Those scowling Russians can be intensely emotional.)

In serious conversation, he professes to prefer his own dilemma to ours. "It is difficult for us, especially in the outreaches like Siberia and Central Asia. No Bibles, no churches—but we survive. With us, the choices are plain. But from what I know of you, the choices seem insidious. Materialism among us is an ideology. We can combat it. But with you, it seems to be a way of life. Your battle, it seems to me, is the harder to fight." If you pray for Yuri in his struggle, remember also that he prays for you. Yuri's choices, however difficult, have not involved him in radically open declarations of faith.

I first saw Olga at vespers services in a central Russian city. Her dress drew my attention. Though it is common for young believers to dress simply—babushkas or shawls for the women and nondescript, coarse dark coats for the men—Olga was dressed in a modified nun's habit with a long dark dress and a veil pinned beneath her chin. She clutched in her hand a long black staff. Crossing herself, bowing deeply through the long litanies of the evening service, she was known to the other worshipers and frequently interrupted her devotions with a smile to one, or a few kisses, Russian style, to another.

Olga is a "nun in the world." With opportunities to enter the monastic life severely limited, this becomes an option in Soviet Russia. Although she was educated for a clerical profession, her radical choice to be so open a believer has committed her to another way of life. She is content in a menial job, that of a street sweeper, which occupies her early morning hours. She is able, then, to attend the daily liturgies that take place in most Orthodox churches in the Soviet Union. Though she punctuates her conversation with signs of the cross and expressions of faith, she is a product of modern Soviet education. She has willingly taken upon herself the contemporary equivalent of an ancient Russian choice: to become a "fool for Christ," a poor person, a pilgrim who gives to others her testimony to the fullness of the Spirit.

These younger believers exist in increasing numbers. Many of them are, in a sense, converts to the faith of their forebears. Most of them were once "good Soviet kids" who, like many of us, found emptiness in the world.

"The Party gave me an appreciation for justice, but it failed me in spirit," said Volodya, once a member of *Komsomol,* a youth cadre run according to Party principles. Volodya at one time aspired to the Party in imitation of his father and older brother, both Communists. He eventually, at 24, turned to the church instead. "I accept, still, many of the political principles—to be a capitalist and a Christian involves contradiction I couldn't bear," he protests. "But I came to the church to find food for the soul. My father and my brother, of course, can't understand. They think I'm in another century. But my grandmother and uncle," he smiles, "think it's great."

Volodya's close colleagues at work know he is a believer and respect his convictions. "In socialism we achieve many goals," he professes, "but without God, we cannot hope to penetrate the center of justice."

To go to confession in the Soviet Union brings into sharp focus the nature and trials of being a Christian. In a mid-sized provincial town during a month-long trip one recent summer, I went to confession to a very busy priest who had just finished a long line of baptisms. You must understand that confession for an Orthodox Christian is of two kinds: frequently we receive absolution, simply a cleansing acknowledgement of forgiveness, before we receive the Eucharist. Much less often, we engage in a prolonged, private face-to-face confession. I had chosen to go to private confession.

The first question the priest asked me, not recognizing me as an American, was: "Did you ever deny God or deny your faithfulness to him?" The question was in an offhand drone. Clearly, it was a question of great frequency. When I said I had not, the priest raised an eyebrow and scrutinized me more closely: "Are you from another republic?" (He expected me to be from one of the Baltic republics, perhaps, where the situation of believers is somewhat less constrained.) When we settled into the details of my spiritual life, he gave me kind, patient, and good counsel. In the midst of our talk, however, he sniffed the smell of tobacco. "Do you smoke?" he asked. I nodded—to my knowledge, our faith did not prohibit smoking. "No more," he said. "Not here in Russia. You are a believer." Going without nicotine was my pathetic reflection of the hard choices Russian Christians make.

The situation of believers in Russia is a complex, many-faceted tale. By no means is the Orthodox Church in Russia a hotbed of dissent. Nor is it a cowering reflection of Kremlin policy. It is an expression of God's kingdom, not ours. And intemperate, righteous indignation at the situation of believers in Russia can hold the church hostage.

Of course the state resists the faith. The state openly espouses an atheist doctrine. We cannot forget that, any more than we can forget that our own state espouses materialist, self-aggrandizing principles no less hostile to faith. Yet to use believers in Russia as ammunition in a propaganda battle endangers our brothers and sisters there as much as anything else.

We should encourage our American press to silence its stridency. We should quell our righteous indignation and listen quietly for a moment to what these believers can teach us. First of all, they can teach us the soul of ecumenism. Orthodox believers, without sacrificing who they are, express love for other Christians.

Vilnius, a city in Lithuania, has a strong Catholic presence and a working Orthodox monastery. There is a profound sense of community among Christians in that vigorously believing city. One gracious woman, a devout Catholic with a deep devotion to the Orthodox St. Seraphim and a smiling portrait of John Paul II pinned up in her kitchen, is the focus for a small community of sharing believers. When I asked her why a mutual friend in Moscow had thought she was an Orthodox Christian, she chided me, "My dear, in Vilnius I was born. Here I am a Catholic. But Moscow is an Orthodox city. Wherever we live, we are God's workers." When I reminded her that bishops, Catholic or Orthodox, might object to her idea of faith by geography, she waved the reminder away with a spoon. "I love our bishops," she smiled, "but I also know human nature. It is divine nature we must obey."

Russian believers can teach us something about a Christian stance toward disarmament. No Russian Christian I know sees nuclear arms as anything but the work of Satan. There is no self-excusing justification among them for a balance of terror. It is revealing to worship with those who feel threatened by us in the United States. When American missiles point at a friend and his children, it is difficult to argue, "Hey, that's O.K. Remember, we're the good guys."

Despite the antireligious bias of their government, Russian Christians see our government as a danger. They are acutely aware that we are the party who actually used the bomb, who will not promise not to do it again, and who see them, after all, as its primary targets. The Soviet press publicizes, accurately, the statements of Christian nuclear apologists. When Jerry Falwell speaks, he creates for Soviet Christians the model of a Christian pastor who would hold over their children the threat of incineration.

I can only imagine the response of my friends in Moscow if, before Sunday liturgy, they read in *Pravda* the publicized words of that great theologian, Phyllis Schlafly: "The atomic bomb is a marvelous gift that was given to our country by a wise God."

And finally, Russian believers can teach us something of the spirit. Simplicity, purity, a willingness to become "fools for Christ"—these are qualities we could use ourselves. In Russia, where being a Christian involves an irrevocable break with success, I believe that we find a lot of very good and wise Christians. Respectability can undermine the radical injunctions of our Lord. Russian believers can resist without stridency, persevere without the image of worldly victory that sometimes tempts us Christian activists in our political and religious struggles. In their long-suffering, they can humble us and teach us.

In my discussion of Orthodox believers, I in no way wish to detract from the struggles of evangelicals in the Soviet Union. But I do wish to argue that it is the intense hostility between our two countries, and the hatred which we so glibly fuel, that embodies an evil greater than that contained in either one of us.

In explaining the differences between Eastern and Western Christians, I remember what an earnest young Orthodox physicist said in a small discussion among Catholics and Orthodox, late at night, in one of the vast apartment complexes on the edge of Moscow. "You in the West, it seems to me, aim somehow for the breadth of the gospel. In worship, in social movements, you seem to want to stretch outward. We Orthodox here in Russia are more vertically oriented. We strive for depth, we 'dive' for the spirit. We try to find that center from which radiates the divine energy."

The two movements, vertical and horizontal, create of Christendom a vast and saving cross. May we be as faithful to our role in its work as the believers in Russia are to theirs.

# 6

# From Russia with Love

## *Jane Bernhardt*

My purpose in going to Russia with a peace delegation was to bring home faces and to touch lives. These things I have done. Incredibly, I was welcomed and embraced by strangers in many diverse places. I have sketches of Communists, dissidents, artists, professors, and sanitation workers. I also have many beautiful photographs.

Meeting these people in the Soviet Union has changed my life. Because of the way I was able to know and love them, they are a part of me now. Hopefully, their faces will say what many ideological arguments cannot.

It is my belief that we must love or perish ... and that the death produced by unlove denies us life even now in invisible increments. It doesn't wait until the dreaded event of nuclear confrontation.

Dwight Eisenhower has been quoted as saying: "We must bring the family of Russia closer into our circle. In this way, I believe, is the truest path to peace." I am grateful to have had an opportunity to do this, and hope to share it with as many people as possible through my diary and drawings.

### June 27, 1984

Outside the hotel, downtown, we see lines—the infamous Russian queues, or waiting lines. They are real. It is hard to see us as sometimes the ugly American tourists, demanding of others what we feel is our due (God knows why) when most of the world doesn't have these things. Even on the black market, many things simply don't exist in the Soviet Union.

You don't see much garbage here—no visible advertisements, although there are numerous political posters.

Moscow has a slightly mournful quality. Ancient grandeur had its price of decadence, privilege and repression, but remove privilege—remove some of the ambition and incentive—and you have a people unable to rise to the creative peaks of the past. What is new is functional, not beautiful. What is old is beautiful beyond belief. In between is a gap of sadness, perhaps inutterable disappointment, not to mention sacrifice.

But there is so much I haven't seen. The warmth of people on the street is amazing when we need help. Most not only help but also take your hand, smile, and laugh at clumsy efforts to communicate.

In part I think this openness is due to greater safety on the streets. Conversely, the deep silences and unspoken negations that chill one to the bone from time to time are due to the same police efficiency: a protectiveness that evokes both safety and, at a deeper level, fear.

## June 29

[Peter is an artist I met while we were sightseeing in Moscow; unexpectedly, we met again in the metro. We were able to get together several times for long walks in the city. Cveta is a lovely young restaurant trainee whom I observed and drew while in Moscow. We spent several days together there, and I later visited with her family in Kiev.]

When I first saw Peter painting in the convent, I felt an immediate sense of respect: This was someone to be quiet around. As I watched him work, I thought, "This is the man I want to know here." His work was good—sensitive and rather impressionistic—not the glib commercial product usually found at tourist spots.

As Cveta and I were setting out for an evening in Moscow, there emerging from the metro was Peter—and I was incredibly surprised and happy to see him again. After a time of laughter and confusion (he must have changed his mind about wherever he was going, too), we decided to set out all together—Peter leading us on an artist's tour of Moscow. Through his eyes I began to taste its peculiar richness.

Educated as an architect, he knew the history and colorful details—where Pushkin was married and the Tzars kept their horses. Through him I began to touch the soul: the pungent, reverent beauty that seeps through ancient stuccoed walls . . . a sense of history deep in the streets . . . a remembrance of suffering and grandeur.

It was strange to walk with Peter, feeling such kinship, then to look at the magnificent onion-domed churches and monuments rich with history and feel that they were his. How casually he carried such a legacy.

I tried to talk about home. New York—not like Moscow—more noise, more garbage, more business . . . but I love New York. Moscow closes down at night. Peter walks or paints or goes to a friend's house and listens to music.

He and Cveta both said that next time I come they will have learned English to talk with me. I said I should improve my Russian but both said no—they should learn English. They wondered if it was difficult to leave my country. I said no, it is not difficult but very expensive. They said it was difficult to leave their country.

Peter wondered, seeing my cross, if I were Catholic, and I said no. But finding no word in the dictionary for Protestant, Episcopalian, or Anglican, I said simply, "I love God very much." He smiled.

I am remembering all the time spent with Cveta and Peter. How can it be that now I am so sad to leave Moscow? Seldom in life are such deep connections made so quickly.

## July 4

[Professor Litvin is an economist who participated in seminars with peace groups during their Volga River cruise.]

Over dinner, Professor Litvin kept asking me probing questions; what had I thought of the seminar today . . .

what do I think of socialism now . . . the Soviet way of life? I told him I had felt tired and had left the seminar early— also that I was hearing a lot of talk that his system was superior to ours, and I was growing tired of it. He wondered if I believed any of what they were saying and I answered: "I don't know."

"It isn't even a question of convincing me—in some ways I am an intermediary. The people I will return home to address are far more suspicious than I, and I must ask the questions they will ask on my return—regarding Poland, Afghanistan, arms sales around the world . . ." Of course, he gave tight and logical explanations for each of these, but I had to observe that my administration gives virtually the same excuses for military interventionism. A few words differ, but the logic is the same.

He felt tired, I think, and ended by saying he hoped I could report that the Soviet Union isn't so bad—not that they are perfect but that they aren't so bad.

## July 6

What can compare with hazy pink-grey sunsets painting the sky over the Volga—cattle grazing on lush hillsides sloping to her shore?

As we sat on deck, watching the countryside together, Professor Litvin began to speak to me from his heart: "You know, tonight I will probably stay awake all night and think about this cruise and the people of your country I have come to care for—I'm like that, I care deeply very quickly. And I will feel sorrow and I will be trying to find ways of making détente so the skies can be clear for our children."

## July 6

[Alexei (Alosha) is a college professor who for 15 years has been involved in peace work in Leningrad. His doctorate is in American history; his specialty now is political science.

Alexei feels that poor education and communication are major contributors to current tensions. During his lecture to us on the cruise, he said, "There is a saying in Russia: The less you know, the better you sleep. Many people live their lives this way."]

There is a deep double standard here: They fear us and they love us for our power. Alexei says the university students are disgruntled because they don't have the fine cars and clothes and conveniences of our country—that the weapons menace isn't as real to them as these material discrepancies. Here on the boat we meet the party loyalists, the faithful communist idealists who present a solid front and confront us on our nation's aggressive policies. I have been humbled by it (and challenged by it) and have at times wanted to embrace some of these precious children I see on the streets and in pioneer camps and say: "I will do all I can to protect your future—I have never meant to frighten you."

When they see American films (which are very popular) they see that which is better, faster, more beautiful. Hence when we come over they show us the finest that they have—as if they were embarrassed to let us see the underdeveloped reality. When I ask for admissions of humility, they point to economic inferiority with lengthy explanations. But that is not the culpability I am referring to at all, but rather arms sales and intervention all over the globe—like ours. As one they disavow any guilt: Whatever they do is for freedom and justice. If I knew the facts I would understand.

## July 9

After quite a farewell party on the boat last night, Alexei and I took a long walk at late sunset along the water's edge. I felt such a part of the quiet night and the Russian people we passed; the mist of confusion inside has settled deep into my being like an anesthetic, calming me. Somehow there was nothing to know: a feeling of sadness at leaving the Volga, closeness to the friend at my side. But also fear: that nameless threat trying by any means to puncture my tranquility.

I ask Alexei a thousand questions and he—sincere, intelligent—answers. I ask about dissension, persecution, communism, religion... The answers are candid and enlightening, but the strange feeling remains that I am collecting pieces for a puzzle, but it isn't the puzzle I had been trying to solve.

On July 7 we had a press conference in Moscow. Correspondents from ABC, CBS, *New York Times, Newsweek,* the Associated Press, the *Chicago Tribune,* and other journals were there. Their Soviet counterparts were there also but were silent.

After two days, I was able to write about it.

I have been hit by a Russian taxi traveling rather fast, have entered into costly relationships with three Soviets, have had wrenching debates with experts over Soviet policy, have experienced some of the darkest sides of the system (fear that left me shaking for hours) . . . All this and more I have experienced in a short time here, but nothing has succeeded in shaking my fundamental human orientation, nothing has produced the shock that the press conference did. The utterly familiar raises a sword against you, and you are profoundly changed or hurt.

As one voice the American press goaded and condemned us as Communist dupes: our quest not only hopelessly naive but dangerous . . . our impressions false because everything we were systematically shown was a lie, a carefully controlled facade.

We were herded, they said. We saw the people who were prepared for us; we were not led to the poorest parts of town nor introduced to dissidents and drunks. We were not reminded of Soviet secrecy and repression. The sting of untruth is always truth.

The love and honesty of my Soviet friends was not an act. I have been free to wander anytime, anywhere (stay out all night if I choose). A people who wait in lines without access to decent consumer goods, an economy rebuilding against obstacles incomprehensible to most Americans—these are true. Deep warmth and affection have been there beside the grim exteriors and occasional flashes of darkness.

But even all of this is not the point. All worldly power corrupts: no system bears close scrutiny. But our beloved media scrutinizes—it picks the blemishes off the Russian landscape and uses them as proof—fuel for paranoia.

Where are their expressions of humor or compassion, remembrance or commendation? These people died in incomprehensible masses to stem the tide of Nazism. And they remember. They will not be unprepared against aggression. Both sides are aggressive—both sides fear. But the media wizards fuel the fear. They perpetuate the cycle that will end in suicide for all.

## July 14

As I was leaving the Hermitage museum in Leningrad, crossing the Winter Palace Square, I met Sasha. He probably hoped for a trade of some sort—he does a lot of "business" with Americans—but, finding me poor in goods but friendly and curious, he seemed content to share his views on the world. His English was excellent, due to the ten or so years of business with Americans. He was incredibly frank:

"So your Russian peaceworker friends are registered with the government: you call that a peace movement?

"They will tell you everything is wonderful here: that we are a peace-loving people. This is true—the people want peace just as your people want peace. But the government wants to spread its system all over the world. They both do.

"Now every small eruption in some country becomes a microcosm of our ideological struggle: a test of which system wins. We see capitalism as a dying system—biting, lashing out at the end of its era. Deadly. You think we want to spread communism everywhere.

"People can do nothing. The governments, they don't care: they will sacrifice 10,000 or even 10 million people here or there for the sake of their ideology."

I asked him how he could speak this way, and he said lots of people speak this way—he has been doing it for years—you can't put all of them in prison.

I wondered what, if anything, gave him hope. I told him about my faith . . . and my feeling that . . . we must do something, even when it seems hopeless. He answered that he thought the person-to-person work was good; "Show them that behind the propaganda and political differences we are the same people."

*MARINA*
*Intourist Guide*

*VALODIA*
*Engineer, Sochi*

*OXANA*
*Confection worker,*
*Moscow*

*ALEXEI*
*Political Science*
*teacher, Leningrad*

# 7

# A Glimpse into the Life of One Russian

*Scott Neufeld*

Within an apartment complex on the outskirts of
Leningrad lies flat number 252, the home of Alexander, a
Russian. Number 252 is a small room—seven by eight feet
at best. For lack of closet space, a University of Michigan
football shirt and other clothes hang about the walls of
this poorly lit room. The desktop houses an overflowing
bookcase and its surface is strewn with Hollywood gum
wrappers, numerous paperbacks, and *Time* magazines.

Alexander is a 24-year-old blond-haired plumber
who has a hearty laugh and an eagerness to talk with
foreigners. On the blue-gray concrete floor lie a few of his
tools, reminding one of his occupation. As a plumber he is
responsible for the maintenance of 100 rooms in the
apartment complex where he lives. Unfortunately, his
work suffers from a problem often noted about modern
Russian society—lack of incentive. Regardless of how
many hours he spends in actual repair work, his pay
remains the same. There is no "ladder" for him to climb
and no chance for an individual pay raise. "I don't have
here any money. I have only time," he commented, referring
less than enthusiastically to his easy going lifestyle.

Alexander's books dominate one corner of his room,
necessity forcing him to pile them in the bookcase and in
most of the space under his desk. It is not hard to guess
what he does in his spare time. "I like to read," he said,

mentioning Russian novelist Aleksandr Solzhenitsyn as his favorite. "All (of his) stories (are) true." At the time of my visit he was reading Solzhenitsyn's *A Day in the Life of Ivan Denisovitch.* Among the stacks of "quietly obtained" books, was another Solzhenitsyn novel, *The Gulag Archipelago,* which deals with the Russian prison system during the harsh years of Joseph Stalin. *The Gulag* has special meaning to Alexander because his grandfather was placed in such a prison. Alexander did not mention why his "greatfather" was imprisoned, but he did disclose the nature of his own run-ins with the authorities.

One situation arose when an overly suspicious citizen confronted Alexander who had just been speaking with some Americans on the street. The citizen asked, "Why do you talk with foreigners? Do you have a passport?" and then insisted that Alexander accompany him to the police station. After checking his file, the police released him. He said, however, that after a similar experience, he and a friend spent fifteen days in prison, "but," he added with a chuckle, "I'm not a hooligan."

Glancing about the room, one notices a radio on his cluttered bookcase, and another on the floor by his bed. He explained that he used the smaller one as an alarm and the larger one to pick up Voice of America and BBC broadcasts. He acknowledged that in the Russian system information is not readily available. "Only the government can know fast."

Information is also edited for the Russian masses. For example, parts of Ronald Reagan's 1986 New Year's Day message were blocked out. "One minute I listen, five I can't. Two minutes I listen, three minutes I can't."

The media flaws are not, in Alexander's opinion, limited to the radio. "Soviet films are a factory of problems." To escape this, he and his friends occasionally obtain video cassettes of such American films as *48 Hours,* and the *Rocky* and *Rambo* movies. Alexander thought Eddie Murphy was "very funny" but that the Sylvester Stallone films, although entertaining, were "anti-Soviet propoganda."

Despite this "propoganda," Alexander has confidence in the current Soviet leadership. There is a portrait of Gorbachev above his mirror on an otherwise drab wall. He admits that the status quo in Soviet society has many shortcomings. "I think it (the education system is) a garbage of (a) system. There is too much freedom and students don't study." He also mentioned alcoholism as an ever present problem. He feels, however, that Gorbachev is "a new, fresh start for Russia."

A final glance at Alexander's homey room reveals many of the traditional Russian possessions: a fur hat, several painted wooden dolls, and a Russian flag decked with military pins. The military paraphernalia, however, has little relation to his views about peace. "The young people don't want war with your country! It's the government's ideas. It's a very stupid idea of war." His intensity suggested a firmness in this view and, perhaps, a strong belief system from which it was drawn. Yet, amid the clutter of his room, one could find no sign of religiosity. Alexander explained. "I'm (I have) religion. It's not difficult, but too many friends don't like church and religion . . . (so) I have religion in my heart."

# 8

# God Is Still Smiling in Leningrad

## Edith Eckart

On Thursday afternoon before Easter, I stepped out of the Intourist hotel—alone. A cold wind blew in from the Baltic. I clutched the address of the Leningrad Baptist Church in my hand. Down the block was a taxi stand. In a few minutes a taxi with its green light on rolled up to the curb. I handed the driver the address and got in. I tried one of my Russian phrases: *"Vi gavariti pa angliski?"* (Do you speak English?) He shook his head. The silent half-hour ride to the church cost me four rubles (about five dollars). It was a little after six o'clock. Two large Russian charter buses were parked outside.

Stepping inside the church, the interior felt familiar, like Protestant churches back home—plain, with no icons, candles, or priests in gold-embroidered vestments. In contrast, Russian Orthodox church interiors are ornate and gilded. I felt at home in the bright simplicity of the Baptist church.

The activity taking place was not a worship service. The pastor was answering questions asked by a large group of young men seated in the front of the church. Later I was told these were students from the Russian Orthodox Theological School at the Alexander Nefsky Monastery in Leningrad who were learning something about Protestantism. They had come in the buses outside. I didn't understand a word of the exchange. A fit of coughing gave me an escape, and considerate people guided me to a kitchen where two *babushkas* (grandmothers) gave me tea and smiles.

I said my Russian words for "I am from California. I come in peace and friendship." More smiles and calling in of others to greet me. More tea, and a cream cheese sandwich. "Would I have a bowl of soup, too?" their motions asked. I took out pictures of my children and grandchildren at Trinidad beach, and a church in Arcata, California. They smiled and chatted in a universal tongue of goodwill. Someone had gone for the church secretary. Anatoly came in, greeting me warmly in English: "Welcome to the Leningrad Baptist Church. Our evening service starts in a few minutes. It is two hours long. Can you stay? I will translate." He wrote his name, and the address of the church in my notebook and said, "Please have the Christians in America write to us, or visit us if they come to Russia."

I took notes as he went on: "Thirty converts will be baptized on Saturday. One hundred baptisms in the past year. Yes, we have Bibles, but not enough. Some people have to wait. Billy Graham preached here to 1,500 people in the church and another 1,500 people in the street outside." We returned to the sanctuary. A choir of forty, twenty men and twenty women, sang a vigorous hymn. Prayers and fervent testimonials came from the congregation and there were solos and duets, all rich with the spirit of Christ.

Anatoly leaned over to me: "Would you like to give a message to the congregation?" (Oh, God, how I wished I could speak their language and give it directly.) Out came a sheet from my notebook. I wrote a greeting from the thirty-nine members of the group I was travelling with, The Earthstewards. Our mission was entitled "To Russia With Love." We had fifteen children with us, including my grandson. I wrote of the many Christians in America who wished them well and who were working for peace between our countries. Anatoly translated my message and passed it up to the pastor.

The sermon was an admonition to be steadfast in devotion to Christ. "We live in dangerous times for our planet," he said. "Our Christian devotion must empower us to be strong. By our lives we show the portrait of Jesus. People see this." On the white, well-lit walls were these words: "God is love." and "We preach Christ crucified, resurrected, and coming again."

Then came a rousing hymn and some announcements, meetings scheduled, and my message was read. A hundred faces swing up to smile at me where I sit in the corner of the balcony. I see love, goodwill, and hope in their upturned faces. My heart bursts with love for them, and my eyes spill over with tears.

Later Anatoly says, "May I tell you how much we needed your message of love? You see, only yesterday our newspaper reported that your Congress had voted funds for MX missiles. Many people are frightened and in despair. God bless you for coming."

Anatoly called a taxi for me. We hugged and kissed the three-cheek kiss. (Men do this with men, too, in Russia.) I rode back to my Intourist hotel in quiet, with an ambivalent mixture of joy and grief.

At breakfast I shared my adventure with my tour group. We formed a peace circle in the lobby and sang "We are the world, we are the children . . ." which was to become our theme song in the next two weeks. My Jewish friend, Brad, took me aside: "Tonight is Passover. Will you go with me to the services at the synagogue?" And so we were two together as we sallied forth on my next spiritual adventure.

Within me, I know, God is still smiling in Leningrad.

# 9

# Books, Bibles, and Blood Banks

## *Clyde Weaver*

Every two years in September, over 200 thousand Soviet citizens make a pilgrimage to the Moscow International Book Fair. These book lovers wait in patient lines hoping to get a glimpse, at least, of some of the 200 thousand books on display from over 100 countries. As these book addicts gather, one detects a quiet sense of awe and almost reverence. Approaching the book exhibits, their patience is rewarded. Not deterred by a pushing crowd, they carefully peruse this world-wide menu with the anticipation of hungry diners.

"Books for Peace and Progress" is the slogan for this third largest book exposition in the world. Enclosed by the massive buildings of Moscow, this fair reflects a reading population with its 4500 city libraries. Politics somehow seems irrelevant when one encounters such intellectual vigor. As the Soviet people are met in this human drama, one shifts to a different perspective on propaganda—both Soviet and American. Why do we try to build bridges on military might? Books and the emotions they stimulate could build a more permanent bridge with ideas competing instead of missiles. The printed word promotes dialogue. Peace and books need each other.

One of my fellow American publishers tried to sum up his feeling as he entered the United States. "It's those crowds that haunt me. I feel like embracing that whole

gentle mob that came and waited and accepted and sacrificed and endured—because they love the printed
word."

This excitement for literature was never more evident
then in the booth representing spiritual life and religion
from the West. As crowds gathered, there was a sense of
the mystical. In spite of seventy years of aggressive atheist
teaching, a strong Russian religious legacy persists. The
church has not faded away. Although monitored and re-
stricted, its vitality outlives its detractors. A large Russian
Bible featured in the Protestant booth was easily the fair's
most popular book. Its rich leather cover, gold-edged
pages, and silk inside trimmings gave this document a
special uniqueness. As the crowds reverently surrounded
it, the word among visitors quickly defined the area as the
"Bible Booth." Some would kiss it; others copied from it.
It was photographed, read, touched, and held. A ten-year-
old quietly stood by it for over an hour without speaking a
word. A visitor inquired of my colleague how many Bibles
he had in his home in America. After counting up to thirteen, our Soviet friend said in astonishment, "Thirteen
Bibles! And I can't get one." He then forthrightly suggested, "with all those Bibles, you Americans ought to be better than you are!"

A Lenin library official checked on the displayed
Bible's authenticity. A language teacher informed us of its
"Old Russian" alphabet. Artists marvelled at its calligraphy.
How interesting to find so much excitement for a book
that for seventy years has been put down, taught against,
and vilified by a system that is seeking its salvation elsewhere. There seems little doubt that the Soviet society
must accommodate what it cannot confirm. The "Russian
soul" is so intertwined with the religious tradition that
communism will need to continue to find ways to respect
its existence without acknowledging its ideology. While
the battle lines are clearly drawn for the Soviets, much of
our western Christianity has a different problem. Here
both the ideology and the existence of the church is
accepted—indeed, encouraged—but isn't it possible that

while our Soviet neighbors are hindered with too little religious freedom, we in the west are hindered with too much? Is not godlessness a problem inherent in both societies? This common enemy, whether due to functional atheism or professed atheism, is a focal point around which the church in both societies can and must rally.

Before leaving Moscow and the book fair, with its many written and spoken words, I felt constrained to communicate my faith in a different way—by giving a pint of blood. It was only after many attempts by my interpreter that he finally reached the Moscow offices of the International Red Cross. I was instructed to take a taxi to the Central Institute of Hematology and Blood Transfusions, a 140-bed facility. When we arrived, we were greeted at the door by a woman doctor. "Are you Mr. Weaver?" she inquired. After confirming my identity, she indicated that a problem existed. "A problem?" I asked. "In America they are very anxious for all the blood donors possible." Then she said, "You are only the second American to ever give blood here." Slowly I began to realize my lack of planning ahead and told my interpreter to inform the authorities of my intent in this gift to our Soviet neighbors. I was then ushered into a room with an English-speaking representative of the institute. After an interesting one-hour discussion, the doctor returned and informed me that I could give my blood.

Without any documentation concerning my blood type, present state of health, and so forth, I needed to have a physical examination. I was taken to a room and put through a series of tests for heart sounds, blood pressure, and reflex responses. During the blood pressure test, I had a moment of anxiety. My blood pressure was too high. We decided to try the other arm. I closed my eyes and tried to relax. This time I passed! Next we went to a large area filled with contour chairs. By this time the word of my presence had passed through the grapevine and a small group had gathered. As my blood filled the plastic bag by my side, I had to think of the terrible waste of life that this country experienced during the second world war—20 million casualties by some estimates. It is no wonder that peace is such a regular part of their conversations with Americans. Lastly, we moved to a small dining room where eight to ten medical personnel talked to me during the customary post-donation meal. I was presented with two pins signifying my donation, and other gifts. When we finished, I asked my interpreter to read a short statement I had written to try to explain my "blood gift":

> *Dear Friends:*
>
> *I am giving a pint of my blood as a way of making a statement of dedication to life and world peace. On a planet where war and violence are so prevalent, death can become too casual. But the miracle of life is never cheap. Our creator endowed us with an intricate and marvelous body that needs tenderness, not hate. The soil of your nation was drenched with the blood of your people during the great patriotic war. It is my hope that we can give our blood for life, not death; that we can build blood banks for hospitals, not battlefields.*

As my interpreter concluded, some persons applauded while others appeared on the verge of tears. I was overwhelmed by the recognition that probably everybody around the table had lost a loved one during the war.

As we were leaving, Dr. Nakarova, the head physician of the institute, said, "Mr. Weaver, wouldn't it be wonderful if the leader of your country and the leader of our country would give their blood, have a meal together like this, and talk about peace."

In retrospect, I continue to believe that symbols often speak louder than words. As we relate to our Soviet neighbors, and they to us, we need to find new ways to say we care about each other. Our differing systems must not keep us from experiencing our common humanity.

# Grass-Roots Diplomacy: Reconciling the Superpowers

## Richard Deats

A *New Yorker* cartoon pictures two men talking at a cocktail party. One asks, "What would you think of the Soviet Union completely disarmed?" The other ponders a moment and then replies, "I'd say it is not enough."

Our problem is that we haven't expected anything but bad news from the Soviet Union. The atmosphere has been so charged that we have looked for the worst—and usually gotten it in a kind of macabre self-fulfilling prophecy.

Nowhere is our mind-set better illustrated than in what happened August 6, 1985, the fortieth anniversary of the bombing of Hiroshima. Mikhail Gorbachev announced on that date that, as an act of good faith, the Soviet Union was unilaterally suspending all nuclear-weapons testing until January. He invited the United States to reciprocate.

The Reagan administration refused, arguing that the Soviets were suspending such testing only because they didn't need any more, having just finished a big series of underground explosions. According to the US Department of Energy, which monitors such things, the Soviet Union had indeed carried out seven underground tests in 1985, all prior to the moratorium. But that was only part of the story, for the United States, again according to the US Department of Energy, carried out *thirteen* nuclear tests in 1985, almost twice as many as the Soviet Union.

Two weeks after the Soviet Union's unilateral moratorium on nuclear testing, the United States announced that unless the Soviets did "something concrete" to demonstrate a change, the chances for peace were slim . . .

The November 1986 summit provides hope that the relationship of the United States and the Soviet Union can be changed. But the lack of any concrete agreements affecting the arms race still reveals how dangerous and difficult the road to peace is.

What then can *we* do to turn around this alarming superpower relationship? To create the kind of climate in which governments can more fruitfully meet and agree, more and more people from East and West are engaging in what is known as "grass-roots diplomacy." They are responding to President Eisenhower's insight of many years ago, that "some day the people of the world are going to want peace so much that the governments are going to have to get out of their way and let them have it."

To that end, the Fellowship of Reconciliation and Manchester College in 1985, sponsored another of their "Journeys of Reconciliation." For twenty-five days, forty-four Americans visited Eastern Europe and the Soviet Union as a concrete step in peacemaking on the citizen level. It was a journey I won't soon forget.

In Moscow we met with leaders and members of the USSR-US Friendship Society. Presiding at the meeting was Vladimir Posner, the person who has hosted most of the eight Space Bridges—those satellite hookups between US and Soviet cities in which audiences of both countries sit before giant screens as if they were in the same auditorium with their counterparts on the other side of the world. These Space Bridges have been shown throughout the Soviet Union to delighted audiences; unfortunately, the networks in this country haven't thought them important enough to carry—with only a few small PBS channels bothering to telecast them.

Posner said to us, "Great changes can come in history, even involving things thought unchangeable and

God-given, just like one day slavery was abolished." He believes that the horror of nuclear weapons—and the threat they pose to the future of the planet—will eventually bring about their elimination.

"Some people say that these people-to-people efforts are not significant," he told us. "They insist that only government-to-government efforts are really important, that things like the Space Bridges are only drops in the bucket. But enough drops in the bucket will produce a bucketful."

And that is what our visit was about: drop after drop of reaching out to officials, peace people, church people, ordinary folk in the Eastern bloc, helping to create that paradigm shift that must come in our awareness and perceptions. Attitudes must change; trust must be built on both sides, spreading like leaven across the globe.

The forty-four of us traveled by bus and plane and train through cities, towns, and rural areas. We met with friendship groups and peace committees. We worshiped in trains and in hotel lobbies, in a cathedral and on a hillside. We met young people in a youth center and took long walks with them. We visited a school and heard the pupils' songs and poems for their first foreign visitors. We went to monasteries where for centuries pilgrims have sought oneness with God. We ate marvelous Russian ice cream, drank kvas, and relished the long summer days of the far north. We cheered exuberant Georgian dancers and melodic Ukrainian folk singers.

At a day-care center in Volgograd (formerly Stalingrad) we were given a beautiful program of songs and dances by some of the children. Later we took a tour of that breathtaking facility, with its playground and gardens, swimming pool and gym, puppet theater, small birds and animals (cared for by the children), and a miniature traffic course for tricycles and pedal cars. The director helped us plant a peace garden of zinnias and marigolds, and before we left we sang several peace songs together.

We had long visits with the Group to Establish Trust, an independent peace group in Moscow. Over cups of steaming tea and Russian cakes, we learned of their valiant efforts to build trust between the two superpowers. We were saddened at the mistrust they have met with, not only there but here. The effect of decades of Cold War lies and suspicions is not easily erased. We met Jewish refuseniks, still hoping to get visas to emigrate. We talked to soldiers, workers, and market vendors.

With us we carried twenty-two ribbons from the great Peace Ribbon that had been wrapped around the Pentagon in the summer of 1985. These we hung from our train and bus windows and unfurled in all our meetings, leaving at least one in each city as a reminder of the growing desire of American citizens for a world at peace. We gave a peace quilt made by a group in rural Oregon to the Children's Art Museum in Armenia. We made origami peace cranes and gave them to children on subways and in parks, each Japanese crane a prayer that Hiroshima would never happen again.

In Moscow we visited Spasso House where Donna Hartman, the American ambassador's wife, has made her home a place "where the arms race can be set aside." The ambassador's residence is a grand place turned over to the United States by the Soviets when Franklin Roosevelt extended diplomatic recognition. Donna has opened her home for jazz concerts, American movies, weekly lectures, and aerobic dances. Here American and Soviet citizens can meet together and learn from one another.

Although the ambassador mouths the Reagan administration's hard line, Donna Hartman continues to reach out to the Soviet people in innovative ways. She has even gone so far as to cut daffodils from her garden and go out onto the street, handing the flowers to passers-by.

On Mamayev Hill in Volgograd, at a monument to the battle where millions of Soviets and Germans died, we wept as we heard "Traumerei" by the *German* composer Schumann—and thought of such suffering and death. Near the giant statue of Mother Russia, we gathered in a circle with our ribbons, singing, meditating, and praying for peace. Then we scattered seeds to the wind as tiny symbols of hope and new life.

At Babi Yar outside of Kiev, where tens of thousands of Jews and other Soviets were massacred by the Nazis, we read Yevtuschenko's poem "Babi Yar" and reflected on the meaning of the Holocaust. Afterwards, some American Jews came up to us and thanked us for helping provide space and time to deal with those terrible memories.

At a meeting in Kiev, a physician and poet named Vitaly Korotych admonished us, saying: "Remember: we are your friends. We want to be your allies. Whatever our differences, they cannot be solved by war." In our meetings with people we often found them fearful, frightened by Reagan's arms build up, especially the Euromissiles and the prospects of "Star Wars." When they found we were for *mir e druzhba* (peace and friendship) their mood changed. They often reached out to us in warm embraces.

One of the most delightful facts we discovered was that thirty tons of ice cream are consumed daily in Moscow! Surely here is common ground for understanding, a freeze that not even cold warriors can take exception to.

In reflecting on the underlying causes of the mistrust between the two superpowers, I am drawn more than ever before to the remarkable contrast between what each society seems to value the most. Here in the United States, we talk mostly about *freedom*. We cherish it deeply. In the Soviet Union, the people talk more about *peace.*

These differences are clearly rooted in the history of each nation. The United States is a relatively new nation, founded principally by immigrants fleeing oppression and hardship, desiring freedom to start a new life. Our Declaration of Independence, our Constitution, and our Bill of Rights all reflect this exaltation of freedom. Freedom to speak, to assemble, to worship as one chooses, the freedom of the press—these are all precious rights sought by the millions who came to these shores. (Unfortunately, native Americans and those brought here as slaves seldom played any part in the dream. But that is a topic for another time.)

In our short history, we have known many wars, yet our land has largely been saved from the scourge of armed conflict; our troops have almost always fought in other lands—the Civil War, now all but forgotten, was the main exception. Geography has blessed us with two giant oceans. These, until now, have insulated us from the devastation of war so common to other people.

The Soviet Union, on the other hand, is an ancient land whose giant plains have been the path, century after century, of invading armies. Over the centuries, Mongol and Tartar, Swede and Pole, Lithuanian, French, and German armies have swept across the Russian plain. Especially traumatic was the scorched-earth policy of Hitler, whose armies burned down everything in their path until they reached the very outskirts of Moscow.

One can scarcely meet a Soviet citizen today who did not lose at least one, or perhaps many, family members during those terrible days. They lost more in the city of Leningrad alone than we in the United States have lost in all the wars in our history.

What the Soviet people treasure most is peace, peace from the horrors of war. In their eyes, nothing has more value. That is why, when you visit the Soviet Union, you hear talk of peace on every hand, just as in this country you hear endless words about freedom.

Not surprisingly, all of these affect the way our two societies talk about, even conceptualize, human rights. For example, I've heard many Americans say, "They have no human rights in the Soviet Union." What they mean is that the people of the Soviet Union don't view human rights as we do. When we talk about human rights, we mean *political freedom:* the freedom to worship and assemble and speak out and read a free press.

But when the Soviets talk about human rights, they are shaped by their experience. This is a land which in this century went through a revolution and all of its aftermath, then suffered an invasion in which whole cities and villages were burned to the ground. So their perceived needs and priorities are different from ours.

One of their most cherished desires is affordable housing. In a country where factories and farms and shops have several times been wiped out, another priority is having a job. The remembrance of war leaves a longing for another universal need: good medical care. And this land which overcame mass illiteracy in this century and now seeks rapid economic development wants all its children to be highly educated. That is why one finds such pride in what has thus far been accomplished in achieving full employment, inexpensive housing, free medical care, and good educational opportunities. These things the Soviet consider fundamental human rights.

Just as we cannot accept the control the Soviet system exercises over its people and the treatment that has been given such dissenters as Andrei Sakharov, so they are dumfounded that a rich country like ours tolerates millions of unemployed, lack of universal medical care, and exhorbitant educational costs. To the Soviet people, these are all gross violations of fundamental human rights.

These differences give rise to much indignation and anger. Both societies need to better understand the other, both need to better grapple with the full meaning of human rights. Each side can teach the other much.

I believe the West's individualism, and the Soviets' collectivism are both extremes, both only partial truths. A society that is just and free will have realized the value of *both* individualism and collectivism—rather than making either into an exclusive political dogma, as is so often the case today.

Every day on our trip we tried to find a time and place to reflect together on our experiences. One day we were meeting on the tenth floor of the Roosia Hotel near Red Square, seated on the rug in a little lobby where two wings of the building came together. We began by singing what had become our theme song, "Peace Is Flowing Like a River." Janet Hershberger, a film maker from New York, then said that two Russian friends had taken her and her ten-year-old daughter, Jenny, to the Moscow Circus, something Jenny especially wanted to do. But when they got there, the circus was sold out. Unwilling to take "no" for an answer, one of Janet's friends persisted till she found the manager and told him the situation. Finally, after much effort, the manager happily took his American guests and their companions to four seats—right on the front row! The lights dimmed, and then, to Janet's surprise—before the circus began, the whole audience watched a film on the danger of nuclear war.

Our sharing continued around the circle. Marion Ross, the television actress, said she and Dorothy Taylor, a pastor's wife, had bought roses for their hotel-room window that looked out on the Kremlin. The roses had drooped the second day, but they couldn't bear to throw them out. That evening, when they came to their room, the flowers were gone. Their initial anger quickly turned to joy when they discovered the hotel maid had not thrown the roses out but had put them in a tub of water in the bathroom. That was enough to leave them freshened up to last a few days longer—a lingering reminder of a special act of thoughtfulness.

Then Marlyn Porter, a New Jersey teacher, said that coming back to the hotel through Red Square she had seen a woman trudging along with a load of parcels, seeming to have the weight of the world on her shoulders. Marlyn went up to her and greeted her, *"Doobre ootra. Mir e druzhba."* (Good morning. Peace and friendship.) She said the woman stopped as she examined the English writing on Marlyn's dress. Her eyes brightened and she greeted her, then asked *"Pacifista?"* *"Da,"* said Marlyn, *"Amerikanka pacifista,"* as they embraced one another. Marlyn commented, "It was as if I was supposed to be at that place at that time to meet that woman."

By the time we finished our sharing, some new-comers had gathered around on the edges of our group, intently listening. Several of them appeared to be Americans. One of them said, "Can we say something? We don't know who you are, but we are very fortunate to have stumbled across your group. We are here with seventy Americans who have done nothing but complain about the tourist facilities here in Moscow and find fault with its people and their life-styles. We, on the other hand, are having a wonderful time and having great experiences. Our companions cannot understand this and say that we are probably communists. In fact, one said he was going to report us to the FBI when he gets back to the States!"

We exchanged addresses and gave our visitors some of the peace buttons and leaflets we'd brought with us. But the incident made us realize how much we had to do when we got home. Although we needed to learn as much as possible, our primary task was not to be experts on the Soviet Union or to have answers to everyone's questions. Rather our task would be to share what we had seen and experienced, opening people to the possibility of overcoming hostility and suspicion. Perhaps this is something of what it means to be a peacemaker. Perhaps this is how we begin to live out the meaning of reconciliation.

Our last meeting in the Soviet Union was with the Ukrainian Peace Committee. Men and women from various walks of life told us about their efforts for peace. We had an open-ended time of questions and answers— and then exchanged peace buttons, posters, and literature. Finally we all joined in a big circle and sang "We Shall Overcome," we in English, they in Russian. We left the next day by train for Prague, knowing that more important than all our differences is the basic humanity we share and our common hope for ridding the world of nuclear weapons and learning to live together in peace.

# Incident in Leningrad

## *Kent R. Larrabee*

It was September, 1982 and the last afternoon that I was
scheduled to be in Leningrad. I had visited the War
Memorial there, the Hermitage, the Summer Palace, a
factory, the Leningrad Peace Committee, a working class
sauna bath, and the seminary of the Russian Orthodox
Church; but I had been procrastinating over the activity
that I was most concerned about—passing out my peace
leaflets. I was a little scared because I wasn't sure what
might happen. I had written the leaflet in Helsinki,
Finland and had it translated into the Russian language
which, incidentally, I do not speak.

Nevsky Prospect is the name of the main street. It was
there, in the heart of the downtown area, that I finally took
one leaflet out of my knapsack and passed it out to a man
who was walking along the crowded sidewalk. He took it,
but instead of walking off with it, he stood right there in
the middle of the sidewalk and read it. I was surprised that
others stopped to see what he was reading and then began
reading over his shoulder. Well, I thought, this is going
pretty well; so, gaining courage, I took the other nineteen
copies that I had with me and passed them out to others
who were walking along.

Within ten minutes, over 100 persons had surrounded
me. I couldn't believe what was happening. I was backed
up against one of the buildings and the crowd had grown

so fast that already the people completely blocked the sidewalk. The atmosphere became electric with interest, curiosity, and concern. I was deeply moved. As time went on, the crowd got larger and larger. They not only blocked the sidewalk, but they blocked part of the street. People would take the leaflet and then gather in a cluster to read it, sometimes going over it twice. Then they would pass it on to another group of people who were waiting. As the crowd grew larger, I realized that I couldn't do anything about it. It was a spontaneous happening, so I just stood there and watched and marveled.

At one point a man, wearing a cap, started working his way through the crowd to come up to where I was standing. Apparently he wanted to shake my hand and tell me something. He was an older man and I found out that he couldn't speak English. But when he was finished, I was told what he had said as we shook hands—"We're glad to know that in the United States there are people who believe in peace as much as we do." I tried to hide my tears.

Ten minutes later, a handsome young Russian fellow, about 23 years of age, also came through the crowd to shake hands with me. He spoke perfect English, a common skill among the younger generation of Russians. He held in his hand a book which he had gone off to buy after he had read the leaflet. He said, "Here, I have a book for you. It is all about my city, Leningrad and it is written in English." Across the fly-leaf he had written "For my American friend" and had signed his name and his wife's name. I shall never forget his warm, eager smile as I thanked him.

Finally, after nearly an hour, the police came. The crowd parted and four officers came up to me. Without a word, they took me by the arms and, putting me in their car, they hustled me off to the police station. They brought me before the head sergeant and the first thing he wanted was to read my peace leaflet. While he was doing that, I took the liberty of emptying the contents of the knapsack out on the table since I suspected they would want to see what I had there. Immediately, they noticed that I was carrying a lot of papers written in English: letters, reports, peace pamphlets, and so forth. They became suspicious and went to the telephone to call in a couple of translators. When these men arrived, in about five minutes, everyone left the large front room of the police station and went into a back room, presumably to try to figure out what to do with me.

I was left all alone and no one was guarding me. I stood there wondering—would I spend a night in a Russian jail or maybe a week? Would I be deported? I hoped that wouldn't happen; but I had no idea of what was coming. Suddenly it dawned on me that what I needed to do was take that whole situation and hold it in the Light—to turn it over to God and not worry about it. So I sat down in a chair and tried to do just that, meditating silently.

Finally, they came back in and the interpreter came up to me and said "Here are your papers. You are free to go." At that point, I stood up and looking into the eyes of between 15 and 20 officers, I said—"I want to congratulate the police department of Leningrad for doing a good job. You did the right thing. I was causing a big commotion in your city and blocking traffic." Then I paused and said— "I think you have a fine police department."

When I said this, it broke the ice and then they all wanted to shake my hand and they wanted my autograph. It was such a switch. Before, they were being very formal and very serious. But suddenly they became most friendly and relaxed. They told me that when they were in the back room, they discovered some poetry that I was in the process of writing and so they asked the translators to translate my poetry for them. It was the first time in my life that anyone had asked for my autograph, much less my poetry. I found out when I got back to the States that Russian men really go for poetry in a big way—that it is quite important to them.

Then they insisted on taking me in their police car to where I needed to go. As I left we shook hands again and I felt that I had made some good friends with the Leningrad Police Department.

# THE USSR AND THE US

No day
can be as bright
as the day we find each other.

A miracle is born then
of hostile nations
coming through the crisis
of 20,000 nuclear weapons
and mutual despair
to a new paradigm of love,
of love that repents,
of love that forgives,
of love that reaches out
to those who are different,
of love that feels the new energy
when hate lets go,
of love that buries
the weapons of death,
of love that shares,
of love that understands,
of love that embraces,
of love where compassion flows
and men and women everywhere
feel the new order of life.

The day we find each other,
our hearts will rejoice
and tears will be the seal
of our rejoicing.

Today is that day.

# 12

# In Moscow,
# the Subject is Peace

*Jim Forest*

In Russian, the word *mir* can mean both peace and world. *Mira mir* means peaceful world. Appropriately, it is a Mira Prospect number 36, north of Red Square, that the Soviet Peace Committee has as its national headquarters. A few miles to the south, across the Moscow River and beyond the Lenin Hills, in the small apartment of Yuri and Olga Medvedkov, is the center of the Group for Trust Between the US and the USSR—the Moscow Group for Trust, as it is known. Journalistic adjectives have been attached to the two organizations—the one with its own building is "official" while the other is referred to as "independent." The two adjectives mark battle lines. Between the two groups, there is little *mir* lost.

While in Moscow with two co-workers in the fall of 1984—one from England, the other from Sweden—I was able to meet at length with leaders of the Soviet Peace Committee, and toward the end of the stay with leading members of the Group for Trust. Neither group was quite what I had anticipated.

In the case of the Soviet Peace Committee, I expected an overcrowded office in premises that had been new in the days before Nicholas II: something like the offices peace groups squeeze into in the US. Instead I found a modern office and meeting center of several stories erected especially for its present use, its walls handsomely paneled, with spacious rooms and wall-to-wall carpeting. In the conference room where we had a number of conversations, we sat around a circular table with built-in microphones, and—for invisible simultaneous interpreters—a television camera high in the corner that produced a whirring sound as it shifted focus from speaker to speaker. For me, the fine and expensive appointments were not a plus. I prefer churches and peace movements not to lay it on too thick.

On the other hand I expected our host Gregori Lokshin, secretary of the Soviet Peace Committee, to be all ideology and politics, perhaps a bit grim, with a face to match. Surely Communists should look like Communists. Instead he looked like an aging cherub, and had a sense of humor. (I hadn't met him before, though we had been carrying on a busy, often intense correspondence for at least two years on such topics as Afghanistan, Soviet dissidents, the Korean 747 tragedy, conscientious objection, nonviolence and pacifism—a correspondence full of disagreement and argument.)

In our first meeting, Lokshin stressed what he believes is an aspect of Soviet culture which is fundamentally different from US culture and which is so at variance with individualism that Americans often find it unimaginable. "You Americans," he said, "usually say 'I.' In this country, we usually say 'we.' Hard as it may be for you to believe, here nearly everyone has a similar view. Among the vast majority, you will not find differences in principle—rather differences in nuance or shade."

I am not as quick to dismiss this kind of sweeping remark as I used to be, partly because my recent readings on the Russian Orthodox church, including books by both Russian émigrés and by theologians from the West who have come to intimate understandings of Russian piety, have stressed the collective spirit of the Russians and recognized this as something far more ancient than the influence of Karl Marx and V. I. Lenin. Pierre Kovalevsky, in a study of Saint Sergius and Russian Spirituality (1976) notes the oft-repeated generalizations that "the characteristic features of the Russian people are freedom of spirit, a love of pilgrimages, a detachment from the goods of this world, and a revolt against the bourgeois world." He disagrees only with those who "exaggerate the freedom of spirit of the Russian people. Certainly it exists, but it is constantly limited by their sense of community." In my own conversations with priests and theologians in the Orthodox church in Russia, I often heard them use the phrase, "the sin of division."

On the other hand, clearly there is deep division among Russians. It was helpful to hear members of the Soviet Peace Committee teasing each other about divisions of opinion that surface among them—but I was painfully aware of the far deeper and less friendly divisions which have gotten many Soviet citizens into cauldrons of trouble, and which not so many years ago cost millions of lives.

"You have to understand," a Soviet writer told us over a meal, "that it is one thing for us to complain and disagree among ourselves—we do it easily—and altogether different for us to disagree in front of visitors from other countries. Frankly, one of the things that often disturbs us about visitors from the United States is the way in which they condemn their own country. For most Russians, these kinds of statements are a failure in basic courtesy. We try to emphasize the best aspects of our country, and to find some way to explain the worst. It is embarrassing to hear visitors who have nothing to say about their home country but what they dislike!"

Certainly, the Soviet Peace Committee is no complaint society with regard to its own state. It is taxing to hear nothing but positive thinking on any subject, but particularly so in regard to government policies. To be sure, we were aware and grateful for all sorts of offers and initiatives that have been made by Soviet political leaders: the pledge not to be the first to resort to nuclear weapons, the readiness to enter into a freeze agreement, the legal prohibition against war propaganda, the official enthusiasm for disarmament down to the level of brass bands and water pistols, and so forth. Yet, as Lokshin said early on in our conversations, the Soviet Union is no paradise. It will be a step forward in East/West conversations when Soviets feel freer to discuss what isn't at the level of paradise in Russia.

## The 'Official' Peaceniks

The Soviet Peace Committee was eager to convince us that it is not simply a public relations department of the Ministry of Foreign Affairs, and so pains were taken to share with us the Committee's history and its financial structure. It was begun early in the Cold War, in 1949, by people who felt another world war might be approaching and who wanted "a public movement" in the Soviet Union to support steps for peace. Now there are many local and regional groups whose activities include peace rallies and demonstrations, and in recent years quite a number of more specialized peace groups have begun, usually on the basis of professional associations. Physicians for the Prevention of Nuclear War is the best known, but there are scores of others. The money for the Soviet Peace Committee and these other groups comes, we were assured, from private giving, from individuals, unions, special benefits by performing artists and the like.

We had the chance to explore this subject when we visited the Soviet Peace Fund in a mansion on Kropotkin Street that must have been stunning in the gala days of the czars. Among our activities here was to look through some recent receipts and accompanying notes and letters. One was from a local labor union—20,000 rubles representing a "gift day" of labor at their plant. A much smaller gift—50 rubles—was accompanied by a letter from Elena Novika, a 13-year-old girl in the Ukraine, who wrote that "the main talent of a person is to understand other people's suffering as you would your own, for the human race is actually one big family." Her gift was, she said, the result of picking two tons of vegetables at a nearby collective farm. "This comes from the bottom of my heart," she added. "I don't want to dream about Hiroshima."

Similar letters from young donors, though unusual, are not unknown in the offices of US peace groups, yet the habit of suspicion is so deeply ingrained that I wondered if Elena Novika actually existed or had been invented in the next room. Did Soviet workers really offer "gift days" of labor or was this a shift of overtime from which the workers were required to contribute their pay to the Peace Committee? I didn't bother to ask these particular questions—my hosts could no more prove to me their integrity than I can prove mine to Americans who have accused me of being an agent of the KGB. Yet I left the Soviet Peace Fund offices disposed to believe the Elena Novika was real and that there are many people in the USSR making contributions for peace, willingly and at a personal sacrifice.

A few days later, as we were leaving the Soviet Peace Committee offices, two old women walked in looking for someone to whom they could present a contribution which they had collected from elderly people in their neighborhood. The women, both hearty souls, could have been Red Cross volunteers collecting door-to-door contributions in Minneapolis. They promised to collect again and to come back, "next time with even more!"

One of the objections made against the Soviet Peace Committee is that, in contrast to the peace movements in the NATO countries, it seems to make no effort to influence its own government. Lokshin and others associated with the committee argued that while the committee didn't carry on protest activities in front of government offices, in fact it did seek to bring ideas to those in the government and that over the years a number of its proposals had been taken up. The committee had advocated the Freeze long before the government accepted it in principle, for example. Another proposal, that there should be a "lesson in peace" at the start of the academic year in every school had become law—the first national "lesson for peace" day had just happened the month before as a result. The committee's work had resulted in legislation banning war propaganda. There were various other examples.

While we could not be certain how true the claims were, they seemed reasonable. Soviet government policy is not formed by magic. While debate and dissent are less visible than in the NATO countries, they exist; at times, especially in conversations we had with staff of some of the specialized institutes in Moscow, we became aware of wide range of opinion and analysis, as well as differing views as to what approach the government should take. The Russians, including Russians within the Communist party, have not forgotten how to argue. The Soviet Peace Committee—which sees itself as a "public body" rather than a government office—may well be a channel through which various ideas reach the upper levels of the political hierarchy. Possibly there are times when, from the military's point of view, it is seen as a mildly dissident group, or "soft on capitalism." In any event, clearly it is a point of engagement with Soviet society, however different it is from peace movements in the West.

## Patriotism And Belief

It is interesting that within the Soviet Peace Committee, a Religious Circles Commission has been formed in the past year, chaired by Metropolitan Phileret of Minsk and Bylorussia, who heads the Foreign Affairs Department of the Russian Orthodox Church. One of our meetings was with the commission, but in the absence of Phileret, who was at the time meeting with a large US delegation from the National Council of Churches. It turned out that only two members of the commission present on this occasion were believers, Nina Bobrova and Protodeacon Vladimir Nazarkin, though one of the others seemed religiously knowledgeable and might be one of the countless Soviets who believe quietly. Nina Bobrova, a member of Metropolitan Phileret's staff, described the growing emphasis on peace themes in sermons at the Holy Liturgy, similar to what is happening in churches all over the world. She was impressed with changing attitudes in the US in recent years. "Four years ago, I was a guest of Church Women United, and I remember there were people shocked to have a Soviet woman present at their meeting. Now when I am back there, it is entirely different." Professor Yuri Zamoshkin, a department head from the prestigious Institute for USA and Canadian Studies, saw that religious bodies such as Catholics and Quakers are playing a major role in helping many people—not only believers—"restructure our feelings due to the threat of nuclear holocaust"; he contrasted this with the passivity of complicity of religious bodies in violence of earlier times and the recurrent emergence of fascism in "Christian" countries. "The social role of believers seems to be changing radically and in a positive direction."

"And yet," Nina Bobrovna added, "there are Christians in the West who often speak of us as 'the enemy.' . . . This word 'enemy' has specific connotations of hatred and opposition, and this kind of language and thinking can preface war."

Professor Zamoshkin made an interesting distinction between nationalism and patriotism. Patriotism is natural and good, but nationalism is "a kind of group vanity" easily exploited by demagogues who develop the idea of insulted national pride. One of the dangers in the present world situation, he found, is the factor of insulted national pride presently felt in the US and much exploited by militaristic sections of American society, stemming from defeat in Vietnam and humiliation in Iran. The US, he said, feels touchy, vulnerable, and is desperate to prove its strength and resolve. "We in the USSR have to be gentle about these feelings, we have to be sensitive and practice delicacy. We have to renounce all selfishness."

We experienced quite a lot of touchy and vulnerable feelings within the Soviet Peace Committee in regard to the Moscow Group for Trust, a small movement that began in 1982 and whose members have been steadily, though not constantly, harassed, subjected to lengthy interrogations, at times arrested, and in one case (that of Sergei Batovrin) held for a time in a psychiatric ward, a

this though the group's activities have mainly been, by
Western standards, a model of courtesy and understate-
ment. Olga Medvedkov, a woman of minor size, had
recently been tried on the unlikely charge of assaulting a
policeman. She was pregnant at the time of her alleged
outbreak of violence. Happily, following many international appeals on her behalf from Western peace
organizations, she was freed with a judicial warning and
was able to continue her work at an institute of geography.
The Group for Trust often was at pains to stress it is not in
opposition to the Soviet Peace Committee, or indeed in
opposition to the Soviet government or military, but is
simply trying to develop ideas for trust-building steps
which could be undertaken simultaneously by the US and
the USSR.

The formidable Oleg Kharkhardin, vice chairman of
the Soviet Peace Committee, found the Trust Group
mainly a creation of the Western media.

> There is a group, originally with eleven people in it,
> all of whom had applied for exit visas to Israel. . . .
> Their emergence as a political entity in the eyes of
> the West followed a meeting with Western jour-
> nalists who briefed and assisted them. The meeting
> was pretentiously referred to as a press conference,
> but it was exclusively for the journalists who had
> prepared it. . . . The group issued certain publications,
> and two of the members assaulted someone and
> were briefly detained. They wanted to be martyrs but
> were treated as small-time hooligans. . . . In a vast
> country of 270 million people, it is a microscopic
> group meeting in their apartments with a few people
> and some foreign correspondents."

What seemed to have inflamed Kharkhardin in a
special way was a new periodical, *Return Address: Moscow,*
which one of the founders of the Group for Trust, Sergei
Batovrin, had recently inaugurated in New York City, his
home in exile. "Somewhere he has gotten the money for
this. Look at it—if it isn't anti-Soviet, what is anti-Soviet?"
I had seen the magazine already, and had my own distress

about it. Among other items in its crowded columns was a "news" story about a celebration of Hitler's birthday on Pushkin Square, a popular and tranquil gathering place in the heart of Moscow. What Muscovite survivors of the Nazis would do to anyone who dared celebrate Hitler's birthday would probably not serve as an illustration of friendly discourse. Batovrin's journal was typical of the sort of bitter publications that boil up in any exile community—a pity that it should be done, however, in the name of a fragile Soviet peace group. I could only point out to Kharkhardin that Batovrin no doubt had suffered greatly, and that his views were not necessarily shared by those still living in Moscow who were pursuing the principles of their movement and who were pointing accusing fingers at no one.

It was depressing to realize how little real understanding Kharkhardin has of a large part of the Western peace movement, which is quite poorly endowed, often meets in small apartments with few people, and which is also described with contempt by those in the NATO establishment who may see it largely as a creation of journalists who ought to be looking in other directions.

## Competition And Convergence

That evening, our small International Fellowship of Reconciliation contingent of three went to the apartment of Yuri and Olga Medvedkov. Sitting round the kitchen table, we could see the nearby Church of St. Michael the Archangel, beautifully repainted at the time of the Olympic Games but not yet in use as a working church. Souvenirs of many earlier visitors from Western peace groups covered the kitchen walls and the refrigerator door: buttons, banners, even a bumper sticker, *Freeze: because nobody wants a nuclear war.* A television set had a rather neglected look. Yuri sat with his baby Masha on his lap; her older brother Misha was already in bed, but Masha was teething. Yuri is an internationally respected geographer. After Masha went to bed, her place on Yuri's lap was taken by Grasha the cat. "Peace-loving cats of the world," said Yuri, "unite!" Another founder of the Group for Trust was there, Mark Reitman, a mathematician.

Reitman and the Medvedkovs had only recently come into possession of a copy of the magazine Batovrin had published in New York, and were troubled about it because of the contents (many errors and a bitter spirit), because of the lack of attention to positive developments, and because Batovrin had done it—though entirely on his own—in the name of the Group for Trust.

"We exist three years now," Yuri Medvedkov pointed out. "This itself is an accomplishment, as grassroots initiatives are easily crushed. The first reaction to a new movement is to say these people are anti-Soviet. We needed to carry out activities to explain and to show that we are not a threat to the society. Here we are living in a nuclear superpower, a situation in which internal stability is very important, as it would be to any superpower. Therefore we are very much for stability. And the fact is that the situation is quite stable. The majority are content. But it is a situation with many secret police. We see them watching our activities. . . . We have our losses, and it is inhuman to forget them, and so I can understand Sergei is very much preoccupied with this. But the main thing is not to overlook the positive aspects. We have achieved a positive reponse to some of our proposals, some even immediately. When we collected signatures for a summit meeting, with people on the streets signing eagerly, the Soviet press commented there might even be such a meeting before the US elections. We accept this as an indication that our movement is being heard. We have a school of thought about the necessity of grassroots actions, with ordinary citizens building bridges to help reduce the hateful climate that exists, and which is recognized both by ourselves and the Soviet Peace Committee."

Mark Reitman stressed that the group goes out of its way not to be perceived as pacifist or antimilitary—though it is often described as both in the Western peace movement. "I am alive thanks to the Red Army," he said. "This is the army that stopped Hitler's invasion. We Jews would have been the first to die if they had taken Moscow. I would not be here to talk to you. I would have died in the Holocaust."

Discussing the irritation Batovrin's publication had stirred up at the Soviet Peace Committee, Yuri Medvedkov said the Group for Trust has a different view than Batovrin expressed and "always recommends that Western peace groups maintain contact with the Soviet Peace Committee. We provide some competition for the Soviet Peace Committee, but we are not against it. In our society, competition is permitted when the social goal is important enough, such as aircraft design and manufacture. . . . It is good to have competition in preventing nuclear war."

I realized that there were points of convergence in the approach taken by the Group for Trust and the Soviet Peace Committee, especially the view that the development and circulation of ideas is the main social role for peacemakers. "Our work," said Mark Reitman, "is to convert hawks into doves. Some of our papers are read in various institutes. A particular idea or thought or argument may be recognized as good and, put into another paper, makes its way to higher levels and has some influence."

Is the Group for Trust just a new means undertaken by "refuseniks" to at last be given their exit visas? The Medvedkovs and Mark Reitman said definitely not, and pointed out that many refuseniks in Moscow were quite critical of them for what they were doing. "In any event, all of us have withdrawn our applications to leave the country. We now see a reason to be where we are, despite whatever troubles we face as a result." But the fact is that, in the Soviet Union, once you apply to leave the country, you enter into a special category and are seen by many as a traitor. "They want to join with our country's enemies," one Muscovite of mild political views told me, "and so it is hard not to think of them as being enemies themselves." The other fact is that members of the Group are, in many cases, receiving their exit visas and leaving, mainly coming to the US. In recent months, Mark Reitman has been among these. At this writing, the Medvedkovs remain in Moscow.

I left Moscow with real appreciation for both the establishment and nonestablishment peacemakers, aware that the divisions I detected had their parallels among peace groups in the West, though we usually suffer less from the police than our Soviet counterparts.

Did I leave with grounds for hope? Definitely. Despite the many obstacles and dangers, I realized that there is far more dialogue going on in the USSR than we in the West usually imagine. And there are moments of real accord despite major disagreements. I happened to hear one interesting phrase twice, first over lunch at the Soviet Peace Committee, later the same day over cookies and tea with members of the Group for Trust: "We are earth chauvinists."

# A Letter from Moscow

The Peace Forum held in Moscow in mid-February, 1987, included many "stars" among the one thousand attendees who came at the invitation of General Secretary Mikhail Gorbachev. Among them were Graham Greene, Yoko Ono, Andrei Sakharov, Norman Mailer, Gregory Peck, even Kris Kristofferson (star of the American television mini-series, *Amerika)*. There was a blizzard of famous people and many not so famous there. They were divided up into various sections—religious, scientific, medical, literary, artistic, business, ecological, and military.

I was in the religious section, where it turned out I was the only participant (among about 180) working for a pacifist organization. Most were bishops, theologians, and people in important positions in official religious organizations. Christians predominated—the Orthodox

most easily marked because of their attire, though one
readily found Baptists, Catholics, Methodists, Anglicans,
and Christians from other churches. There were also
many Muslims, Buddhists, Hindus, Jews, and Shintoists.
Among those present with International Fellowship of
Reconciliation links were Roger Williamson, director of
the Life and Peace Institute in Uppsala; Paul Kraybill of
the Mennonite World Conference; Lubomir Mirejovsky
of the Christian Peace Conference, Canon Kenyon
Wright, general secretary of the Scottish Churches Council; Michael Harbottle, the retired British general now
active in the World Disarmament Campaign; Dwain
Epps, International Affairs secretary of the National
Council of Churches in the United States.

During most of the Forum, working in smaller
groups, there was free exchange and far more real listening and actual dialogue than I can recall at any other large
peace meeting. People were able to raise all sorts of issues
and questions and complaints without difficulty. (The
press was not allowed in these sessions.) Afghanistan was
often mentioned, and I personally never heard any Russian response in defense of what the Soviet Union has
done there; only repeated statements that the USSR is
busy getting out.

A short declaration, written by a representative committee, was issued from the religious section of the Forum.
The text catches the spirit of the event—neither accusing
nor blaming any government, but concentrating on what
needs to be done if military catastrophe is to be avoided.
"People of religion have special roles to play, among
them: promoting unity among the peoples; increasing
contacts across lines of division; improving the spiritual
and devotional life of human communities; helping to
eliminate prejudiced enemy images; and intensifying
education for peace." Added to these few points was an
appeal to leaders of the nuclear states calling for them to
renounce nuclear deterrence, respect the existing ABM
treaty (thus not to take steps toward SDI or "Star/Wars"
and the militarization of space), and proceed to conclude

new treaties that are concrete steps toward a nuclear-free world. There was an impressive absence of familiar rhetoric in the text, yet it was not lacking in a sense of urgency: "We appeal to all to commit themselves unalterably to the task of building the basis for common security today. The time has come to ask the ancient questions: If not me, who? If not now, when?"

The final meeting brought all the sections of the Forum together for a plenary meeting at the Kremlin, in the Hall of the Supreme Soviet. At last those of us in the religious section were able to meet people in other sections. For the first hour we were together in a large hall in an ancient part of the Kremlin dating back to Ivan the Terrible, then we made our way to the Supreme Soviet. It was striking that there was nothing at all hierarchical about seating arrangements; more than half way back I found myself sitting in front of the one member of the Politburo whose face I would recognize as Georgi Arbatov, director of the Institute for US-Canada Studies. Not many rows in front of us was Andrei Sakharov, about whom the press gathered as if he were Marilyn Monroe risen from the dead, and truly it was startling that this man kept so long in internal exile was now a guest in the Kremlin! Sitting at the front of the hall were people from each section of the Forum, plus Gorbachev.

One highlight of this final session was a speech from the heart, apparently without a note, and with a deeply contemplative note by Graham Greene, representing the writers section. General Michael Harbottle spoke, as did Dr. Bernard Lown of Harvard, one of the initiators of the International Physicians for the Prevention of Nuclear War (with Dr. Chazov, physician to the Kremlin). Paulos Mar Gregorios from India (a president of the World Council of Churches) spoke on behalf of the religious section of the Forum.

Gorbachev was the last to speak. He spoke for about an hour. I didn't realize before he spoke how deep-rooted and solid is his commitment to ending the arms race. Afterwards I left with the impression that Gorbachev is

convinced that there can be no future for the human race
if we continue in the direction we are going and that the
responsibility really is in our hands to make an unpre-
cedented break with militarism and all that it involves—
that our lives and everything that matters depend on this.
He is not a pacifist, rather an abolitionist, but he seems to
have a pacifist's vision of the future, and impressed me as
being prepared to devote his main energies to creating the
conditions for disarmament. If only there can be some
positive response from the United States and other NATO
countries!

Gorbachev also spoke about democratization and
the "revolution now in progress" in the USSR, which he
said was unstoppable and which shouldn't be seen as simply a response to western pressures or criticisms but as an
event with local roots. He stressed here, as he has elsewhere, that the Soviet Union's foreign policy is shaped by
its domestic policy—though one sees that it is not entirely
a one way street and that international goals certainly
influence domestic ones.

Democratization, as I discovered in conversation
with Russians in Moscow and other cities, is one of the
main topics of discussion everywhere. While in Moscow
and Leningrad, I noticed articles in the national press by
people writing, for example, about how they had been
expelled from the Communist Party in earlier years for
daring to say what now is said by the national leaders.
People I talked with spoke openly about formerly saying
what they knew was expected of them rather than what
they felt or believed. There were long pieces in the press
about writers formerly under a cloud. Like Pasternak,
whose censure in the late 1950s by the Writer's Union had
just been overturned by the same organization. Now all
Pasternak's works will be published and his house made
into a museum.

One of the priests in the Russian Orthodox Church,
when asked if there had been changes brought about by
the new reforms in the country for the Orthodox Church
said, "A warm wind is blowing in our country. It hasn't yet

reached the church, but because we believe it will reach us, we are already behaving as if it had reached us."

Dear Friends, how easy it would be to write about this trip for a hundred pages! But I must have mercy on you and simply promise you . . . that I will tell many stories not told here in a forthcoming book.

*CVETA*
*Restaurant worker,*
*Kiev*

# 13

# I Was Taken In

## *Farley W. Wheelwright*

Rule Number 1: Everyone who goes to the Soviet Union for whatever reasons, under whatever auspices comes home an expert in all matters Socialist. I am no exception. Therefore, it is important to be careful what one says and how one says it. Expertise does not imply credibility back at the ranch!

Rule Number 2: Everybody who goes to the Soviet Union for whatever reasons, under whatever auspices takes his/her prejudices with them and inevitably comes home convinced by what they have seen. One generally sees only those things which confirm previously held convictions. I have tried not to be victimized by this rule.

I was never one of those persons who thought that everything the Soviets tell you is propaganda, fed by some gigantic thought machine which originates in a computer buried next to Lenin in the Kremlin. I can smell propaganda whether it emanates from a Chamber of Commerce, the State department, or the Soviet Union. I am fairly expert at rejecting it.

At some point we must develop our own critical faculties. To listen, to observe, to think for oneself, to make one's own decisions are the hallmarks of our faith. These are the rules I tried to apply to the trip Virginia and I took in the summer of 1983 to the Soviet Union in the company of about 150 people. They were as varied a political and theological complexion as you would meet in a Unitarian Universalist Society. I was glad to have most of them as traveling companions.

I had an advantage over most of the group. In 1954 I had taken one of the first tours to the Soviet Union after the second World War, and was bused from Brest-Litovsk through Minsk and Smolensk to Moscow and thence to Novgorod, Leningrad, Helsinki, and home. This was the same route across the Pripet Marshes to Moscow that both the Napoleonic and Hitler's armies journeyed. The countryside had not markedly changed in the past 150 years as far as I could tell.

The return to the USSR this year was like visiting another country. In 1954 the Soviet Union was only starting its recovery after surviving a war that took 20 million lives, and immediately after almost as many more lives in the Stalin purges and the Ukrainian wheat famine. Then none of the country villages had electricity or running water or any other of the amenities that you and I call necessities. None of the cities had luxuries we consider necessities: cars, telephones, private bathrooms or personal privacy.

Twenty-nine years had worked miracles. Now every country village we passed as we cruised down the Don and Volga Rivers had electricity; most had television antennae on the roofs of prosperous-looking farm cottages. Mine was a journey of constant surprise.

I was not prepared to see so many smiling faces; so many healthy babies; so many smartly dressed women with painted toenails and high-heeled shoes; so much prosperity; so little poverty; so much new housing; so many indications of a deeply religious people. These sights were doubly confusing when I considered the skid rows, the crime in the streets, gang wars back home, or the inability of my own government or private capital to rebuild our burned-out urban housing in Watts, Hough, South Bronx and elsewhere, while finding ample funds with which to build glass skyscrapers for luxury hotels, executive offices for multi-national corporations, and banks. The one bank I had occasion to visit in Moscow looked more like a Los Angeles welfare office than a bank. I was treated there with as much courtesy as a welfare client is treated here!

Early on the tour I stopped playing the game of comparing "them" to "us." It is a no-win game. There is no question of being "better than." It is, rather, "different from." We were warned by our Soviet hosts that they live under a different system of government, which affects everything we see and makes comparisons irrelevant. Although the life styles may differ, human natures do not.

In our country we live under a system whose great myth is that everyone has the opportunity to become the President, or at least a millionaire if he or she is honest and works hard. The Soviets live under a system whose great myth is that they live in a classless society, one into which all persons are created equal. Way back when we had our revolution we once had the same dream. Whatever the system of government, human hungers and material fantasies remain essentially the same.

We live in a society in which almost everyone wants an automobile, a computer, a color television and a stereo, a telephone, and two bathrooms in every home. The Soviets live in hopes of acquiring a piano, a color television and a stereo, and one private bathroom in every apartment. All of these wants make Uncle Ivan as much of a materialist as Uncle Sam. There are good reasons why the Soviets are not as car-crazy as we. Cars there are very expensive and the high cost is a way of controlling both consumption and emission pollution. Public transportation everywhere we visited was fast, easily available, cheap, and clean. Few people make a case for the necessity of owning an automobile as is the case with us because our public transport is slow, generally unavailable, expensive, and dirty.

The pervading impression of the Soviet Union which I brought home with me was of a nation longing for peace. Perhaps this was because we were guests of the Soviet

Peace Committee, but I do not think so. Everywhere we went there were signs and posters proclaiming *MIR MIRA MIR*—peace, in the world, peace. Except for the daily English press we did not experience any anti-Americanism. Even the press was more anti-Reagan administration than it was anti-American. They sense the difference between people and leaders.

The major differences between the Soviet government and our government are philosophical rather than actual. Theirs is a controlled socialism, ours is a controlled laissez-faire. Theirs is a so-called closed society, ours so-called open. However, these generalizations do not stand up to close scrutiny. All the labels to which we attach the Soviet life styles: repression, indifference to the needs of the people, communist lies, thought control, and so forth, simply do not fit in with the observations we were free to make on the scene. To be sure, the Soviet system is not perfect. It came as a surprise to some Americans to hear the Russian resource people who were assigned to us freely admit as much. Here are a few things we learned about the Soviet Union which commend it to me, which really took me in:

Full employment. Everybody works, even though many people are underemployed and many people must dislike the jobs they are doing. I thought of our 10 million unemployed, of 20 percent black Americans, 56 percent black teenagers unemployable, and envied the Soviet record. There must be as many underemployed US citizens as there are Soviet. We have this in common.

Economic control means that although few people are well off, everybody gets by. And the few people who do amass fortunes may be farmers, not the nabobs of industry. The average salary in the Soviet Union is 180 rubles a month (about $250.00). In a country where 85 percent of the people are workers or peasants and only 15 percent tabbed as intellectuals one would think that the latter would be smart enough to grade the high-pay people. Rather, the forepersons and certain other workers are the better paid. This observation is subject to better verification than I could make on the spot. Since most women work and there is equal pay for equal work, the average family lives on $500.00 a month which seems to be more than enough.

The dollar figure, however, tells you little. One must count other benefits of a controlled economy. Rent is held to about $20.00 a month, utilities (including the telephone) to about $5.00 more. Transportation costs are negligible (from three to five kopeks a ride—five to seven cents depending on whether you ride the trolleys or the metro), and fares are collected on the honor system. The only cheats we saw were Virginia and myself when we boarded a bus with no change and didn't know how to ask for it!

Another major perquisite to life in the Soviet Union is freedom from worry about health care or education. It comes with residency there. From cradle to grave all medical care is free. From day care centers to post graduate education in the universities all education is free.

Children are a precious commodity which is apparent in myriad ways, both statistically and to the casual observer of kids on the streets and in the parks. In heavily populated republics the average family is two children; in sparsely populated republics more (the Soviet Republic of Tajikistan has the highest birthrate in the USSR with an average family of five children).

Parenthood is the responsibility of the parents, of course, but parents receive special legal, moral, material support from the state. The size of the apartment depends upon the size of the family. Over half the Soviet work force is women, and they are given four months fully-paid maternity leave as well as part-paid leave to nursing mothers until the child is a year old. Working mothers are entitled to shorter hours, a shorter work week and when it can be arranged, work at home. Pre-school centers are vital to the well-being of children as are the marvelous playgrounds which were integrated into every housing project we visited. Children were uniformly healthy and well-fed, well-dressed and happy looking. These observations are in sharp contrast to the 1954 children who lived in circumstances of inadequate food, clothing, and shelter. Everyone in the Soviet Union seems manifestly better fed, clothed and sheltered than they were in 1954. I wonder if we can say the same thing about the United States population.

Surely every visitor to the Soviet Union takes note of its housing. Still in short supply, still looking jerry-built, the massive public housing in this country is a wonder of the world. The Great Patriotic War (World War II) left the Soviet Union devastated with millions of people homeless. Housing was a number one priority and one more talisman of a government responding to the needs (demands?) of the people.

The city of Kiev lost 60 percent of its housing in the German bombardment; Volgograd (then Stalingrad) was totally levelled. Leningrad fared better with a 30 percent building loss but worse with 800,000 dead in a city then of one and a half million people. The Soviet government in the last 40 years has done a gargantuan job building apartment houses. In Leningrad alone there are 50,000 new apartments a month and still there is a housing shortage, and still the people grumble it is not being completed fast enough.

Major complaints are, over-crowding in existing housing and lack of a private bathroom. I talked with a young man in Kiev about his housing. He was 23 years old, a university student majoring in English. He told me he would like to get married but he can't leave his family until they are assigned an apartment with another bedroom for his twin siblings who currently share a bedroom. They must by law be in separate bedrooms by the age of 12 since they are a boy and a girl. If he leaves home before a larger apartment becomes available the family will not be eligible for the extra bedroom, which his father, a university professor, wants for a study.

Another general observation we noted were the long lines and the shortages. Department stores were crowded with people with money to spend but very few consumer goods to purchase. One result of the arms race and the apartment-building boom is a sad lack of consumer goods. There seem to be neither the facilities to manufacture consumer goods in quantity nor the foreign exchange with which to import  them. What there were for sale looked to be of poor quality and little from which to choose. Even in the *Beriozka* shops (foreign currency stores for tourists) the goods are expensive, the choices limited and the quality less than what westerners are accustomed to buy.

The flip side of this observation is that the people are hungry for consumer goods, for the western life styles they see on their television and in the cinema. That the government is trying to respond to the wants of the people is evident. In the local ruble shops cheap souvenir-type products are beginning to appear, imported from India. Even in the *Beriozka* shop I bought a couple of Russian "babushkas" (grandmother dolls) to sell at a bazaar and when I got home was disappointed to read on the label, "Made in Japan." Young Soviet boys will almost sell their souls for tee shirts and blue jeans, young girls their virtue for hair dye and facial makeup. "We adore everything American," a young man told me, "except your nuclear bombs."

In the Soviet Union most everybody looks young, which is hardly surprising with 20 million war dead who, if they were alive today, would be about my age. Whenever I tired of being reminded of that dreary statistic or when I thought of the Stalin-era purges (which are seldom discussed), I had to remind myself that there is hardly a family in the entire USSR who does not have a loved one buried in some mass grave.

Small wonder there exists a Soviet Peace Committee which makes the US peace movement look like kid's stuff. The Peace Committee is supposedly beyond the reach or the governance of the Kremlin leaders. When, like E. F. Hutton in this country, the Soviet Peace Committee speaks, the government listens. In our country we have not commensurately been touched by war. In World War II we lost 500,000 soldiers killed; the British lost 350,000. These figures hardly pale against the grim death toll in the

USSR. A US professor told me he estimated that the Soviet defenses against and ultimate victory over the fascists saved the lives of two million US soldiers. For this there has never been a word of recognition from our government.

The Soviet Peace Committee is financed entirely by volunteer contributions. It is the only autonomous, self-financed charitable organization in the country. This Committee is one way each citizen who supports it can feel she/he has a personal stake in peace-keeping. And it is an active organization. In 1982 more than 60 million Soviet citizens took part in rallies, marches, meetings held during the UN "International Week of Action for Disarmament," the Soviet equivalent of our United Nations Sunday worship service. That week over 12 million signatures were collected and forwarded to the United Nations General Secretary for the second United Nations Special Session on Disarmament. Does this process sound familiar?

Our group was handsomely (I was about to write royally) entertained by Soviet Peace Committees. We participated in a historic first-ever joint USA-USSR peace rally in Moscow. Thousands of Soviet citizens met us at the entrance to Gorky Park where we marched arm-in-arm, to band music and where we gave/received flowers, souvenirs, with tears of joy and happiness as we listened to speeches, sang together, clapped together, photographed each other, and together saw visions of peace between our nations.

The Soviet press and TV covered us and we became known from coast to coast. Everywhere we went people recognized our conspicuous peace buttons, and loved us for our mission to their country. The United States press was invited to attend but failed to show up. The US Embassy in Moscow acknowledged the happening by branding it with two words: "A Fake." Of the rally there was not a word in our mass media.

It is difficult to transmit the intensity of religious life in the Soviet Union other than to say that it is different from religiosity in the United States. All of the Soviet resource people who led our workshops as we sailed down the Don and Volga Rivers were unrepentant atheists. They wore their atheism unobtrusively but proudly. Religion was not much discussed, yet I found the ambience throughout our trip profoundly religious.

People looking for normative Judaism or Christianity found it. While participation in the life of the Russian Orthodox religion is discouraged, it is far from forbidden. The Soviet government has gone to great lengths to preserve and renew the historic grandeur and gold leaf of the great cathedrals. With regard to the Jewish situation, more heat than light is shed by anti-Soviet US propaganda. Jewish members of our tour attended synagogue services. Many of our Jewish delegation traveled independently to their homeland and were warmly received by villagers, Jewish and non-Jewish alike. One of our resource leaders who also was a member of the Soviet Academy of Sciences, was Jewish.

In Moscow, a city of over eight million people, there are only seventeen Russian Orthodox churches open to the public. The great Kazan Cathedral in Leningrad is now the Museum of Religion and Atheism and in *Fodor's Guide Book,* is not recommended for sensitive Christians who would be offended to see displayed atrocities committed in the name of Jesus Christ. Virginia and I attended matins (morning prayers) in Moscow. The music, provided by a pick-up choir was magnificent. The church was sparsely attended by men and women of all ages. The grounds were not well kept and the cemetery was a disgrace, in marked contrast to the secular graves of Soviet heroes killed in the war.

Protestants in our group attended the Baptist Church in Moscow, the same church at which Billy Graham extolled religious freedom in the Soviet Union. There are about five thousand Baptist churches spread throughout the country and about five thousand members in the Moscow church. There are three services each Sunday (how glad I am that I am not its minister!) which I was told are full at every service. Many young people were in attendance.

In the Soviet Union people are as free as they are here not to attend church at all. You can't take the religious pulse of a country by counting the number of people who go to church or temple. How do I know these are a deeply religious people? Let me count the ways:

Their love and respect for nature and protecting the environment. Over 60 percent of the city of Kiev is in parks and gardens for the people. In every apartment complex there is breathing space as well as play space for children, chess tables set out for oldsters. One looks in vain for broken beer bottles, trashing, graffiti.

Their respect for each other. Public places, public transportation are spotlessly clean. In queues people patiently wait their turn. No one seems to jostle another for position in line, even for goods in short supply.

Their care and concern for children as previously noted.

Their care and concern for their dead. Cemeteries are holy places, especially cemeteries for war heroes. Here brides and grooms come after their marriage ceremony and picture-taking. They come in remembrance of the dead and they lay their wedding flowers on graves before taking off for their wedding reception in some rented hall (their wedding rites looked every bit as romantic and middle class as those over which I preside here at home).

Their intellectual curiosity. People read as they ride the subways. Everywhere there are kiosks and libraries (3000 in Kiev alone). The books they buy and/or read are classics, art books, good novels. Many of them are by US authors. Favorites include Jack London, Mark Twain, F. Scott Fitzgerald. Adult book stores in the Soviet are just what they claim to be!

The absence of violence in the cities. We felt perfectly safe to walk everywhere alone at night, on streets, in the parks. If prostitution exists (and I presume it does) the general public is not painfully aware of it. Pornography and violence to women are outlawed.

The people seem to make a religion of peace. As I said previously, the signs are everywhere, *MIR MIRA MIR;* peace, in the world, peace. Peace and the world are almost the same word. There is nothing phony about this religious longing for peace. There is a religious need to express peace. Although no Soviet would use these words, they come tumbling down the ages and reflect what I felt to be the mood of the people in the streets of the Soviet Republics of Russia: "Blessed are the peacemakers, for they shall be called children of God."

What we saw, what we experienced in the Soviet Union was so far from what we read in the US media or what our President has to say about the Soviet Union one is tempted to doubt one's own observations and findings. The questions then are raised: Who benefits from telling lies about the Soviet Union? If our system of government and our way of life is so superior to theirs why must we jeopardize them by spending 44 percent of our national budgeted income on a military complex to protect them? Why in these United States do we not have sufficient resources to look after our own people—our old folk, the unemployed, the sick, the minorities? Are these legitimate questions, or was I taken in and seduced by all I saw and experienced?

Today these questions are rhetorical. Tomorrow they must be answered. While it is perfectly obvious that I greatly admire what I saw in my travels in the Soviet Union, I am not in the least inclined to trade places with Dmitri. I like it here. Had I my druthers I would prefer some sort of a partnership with the best elements of our two systems of governing and controlling the economy, meeting the needs of the people, and most of all finding a road to peace which all humanity could find passable.

Working hand in hand rather than hand on bombs, the USA and the USSR could build such a beautiful world. We need each other for friends, not for enemies. As friends we can learn so much from each other, help each other. That one day we may become friends is my prayer and hope for the future. May it come to pass. *MIR MIRA MIR*—PEACE, IN THE WORLD, PEACE!

# 14

# Mennonites Visit Ancestral Homeland

## Paul Schrag

A group of Mennonites, students and professors from Tabor College, Hillsboro, Kansas, and Bethel College, North Newton, Kansas, visited the Soviet Union in January, 1986. They traveled to such diverse regions as the Ukraine, Central Asia, and Siberia searching out the ancient homelands to which Mennonites had fled from Germany in 1789 to found the "Old Colony" at Chortitza, and later to the Molotschna area, to Traki, and to Old Samara. In the 1870s one third of the Mennonites in the Ukraine left Russia for the Great Plains of the United States and Canada when their privilege of non-participation in the military was revoked. In 1917, at the time of the Bolshevik Revolution, 120,000 Mennonites were living in Russia. Since then many have left, but those who remain are scattered in villages in Central Asia.

An especially memorable moment for the group was the reception of a gift at a collective farm near the Molotschna region in the Ukraine. After sharing the evening meal with them, one of the farm's administrators presented a metal statue, 12 inches high, to Clarence Hiebert, our tour group leader from Tabor College. "This shows a man beating a sword into a plow," said the Russian. "It is a well known symbol of peace." Hiebert responded, "This gift is especially meaningful to us because it is based on a statement in a book that is very important to us—the Bible."

Among the group's most treasured memories are visits with Russian Christians. We visited a Russian Orthodox church in Leningrad, Baptist churches in five cities, and a Mennonite Brethren congregation near Frunze, Kirgizia.

We found the churches packed—in Leningrad scores of people had to listen to the service over loud speakers while standing outside in the frigid night air. We found Christians hungry for spiritual knowledge, asking us earnestly if we had any religious literature to give them. Unfortunately, most of our Russian language Bible commentaries had been confiscated by customs officials when we entered the USSR.

The commentaries we had were the same as those that were dedicated in Moscow, January 6, after the All-Union Council of Evangelical Christians had received government permission to import them. . . . But the customs officials were taking no chances.

Each congregation we visited welcomed us with joyful expressions of Christian love. And we met people of good will, not only in churches and on the collective farm, but also in unexpected contacts on the streets, at public schools and at the University of Zaparozhye, where we spent a memorable evening with the students.

During our stay in Zaparozhye, we took a 60-mile bus trip to the Molotschna area and Chortitza Island. Few Mennonites live in those regions today. The only remaining evidence of their contributions are school and church buildings, a large mill, and other industries, and a few houses.

Going further into Central Asia the group headed for a Mennonite Brethren Church in the most improbable location in the world. Our frustrated taxi driver pulled into an alley barely wide enough for one car, and stopped in front of a tall green fence. We were somewhere on the outskirts of the Central Asian city of Frunze, several hundred miles from the border of Afghanistan and China, and we thought we were lost.

Our group had set out from our hotel in five taxis half an hour before the scheduled 5 p.m. worship service in a local Mennonite Brethren church. We were unprepared for the maze of muddy roads, and each driver quickly lost his way.... But now our driver was motioning to the tall green fence. As we stepped out uncertainly, the gate opened and a man emerged, dressed in a conservative black suit without a tie. When he greeted us with *"Sprechen Sie Deutsch?"* we were astounded to realize that our search had been successful.

The service was already underway, so we walked up the center aisle and took our seats. It was like being suddenly transported into another world. Here, in the middle of a culture of Uzbecks, Kazakhs, and Kirgizians, was a simple meeting hall, hidden behind a tall fence in a narrow alley, occupied by German speaking people with Mennonite names like Wiebe and Reimer who welcomed us as their brothers and sisters in Christ.

The rest of the taxis arrived over the next half hour. The congregation numbered about seventy-five, and included many children and young people. A small choir and six elders faced the congregation. One of the elders formally greeted us, comparing our visit to the biblical story of Joseph being reunited with his brothers in Egypt...

After the service ended it did not take long for enthusiastic visiting to begin. We talked to an elderly man named Jacob Wiebe. His eyes were bright as he smiled broadly, his face marked with lines of a long and difficult life. He spoke earnestly, fairly overflowing with words of Christian love for us. "You are so young," he told us repeatedly. "The future belongs to you." I told him that my ancestors had emigrated from Russia to America in the 1870s. "They could not have known what they would avoid by leaving here," he said, telling us of his family's hardships. He was the last survivor among six brothers. "I wish I could leave with you today."

Approximately 30,000 ethnic Mennonites no longer worship in Mennonite churches, but instead attend Baptist churches which are affiliated with the All-Union Council of Evangelical Christian Baptists, a government approved national Protestant organization under which churches may worship freely, as long as they follow certain restrictions, such as not evangelizing non-members.

Churches flourish in spite of restrictions in remote areas such as Novosibirsk and Frunze, but the situation is more difficult in Moscow, the center of Soviet power. Some of our group visited the only Baptist church which is allowed in Moscow, a city of eight million people.

The ongoing vitality of the churches lends credibility to the feeling that the Soviet government is fighting a losing battle for the hearts and minds of the Russian people. But the "secular religion" of Marxism-Leninism still dominates, as we saw when we visited Red Square in Moscow.

We merged into the huge line to view Lenin's body on a snowy, blustery morning, with the red brick wall of the Kremlin looming above us. In the distance the line disappeared into the mausoleum, a small rectangular building of red granite. Its simplicity is striking among the beautiful architecture all around. An hour later we reached the entrance. Down the stairs, into the cool, black interior, we entered the silent crypt room. Soldiers kept us under close surveillance as we walked around the body at a distance of about ten feet.

Deciding whether the body is authentic or a skillful wax replica, as some allege, is difficult in the few seconds one has to view it. Someone observed that displaying Lenin's body in this way seems an attempt to create an illusion of immortality about him. Among innumerable slogans posted on billboards throughout Soviet cities is this one: "Lenin lived, Lenin lives, Lenin will live."

Our group's best chances for interaction with Russian people came in the churches, where we found that our common identity as Christians instantly broke down international barriers. As we made friends with Russian people, it was sad to realize that powers stronger than ourselves in both countries are working to promote mistrust, even hatred, rather than reconciliation.

# 15

# Roots and Wings

## *Danaan Parry*

Arriving at Moscow Airport after flying exactly half-way around the world is like having the novocaine wear off immediately after the dentist has been drilling your teeth for an hour. *"Pashport, Pajaulustah,"* says the concrete-faced soldier in the steel booth. He looks not at my eyes but in the slanted mirror behind my head. Does he think I have contraband taped to the back of my neck? His grimness seeps into me and I become grim. The whole world becomes grim and I shudder at the thought of three weeks of Soviet grim. I even flash on a life of grim should he decide that I am a spy. The floor will open up and send me plummeting through a tube to Siberia, never to be heard of again.

Next in line is my 14-year-old son, Michael. *"Pashport, Pajaulustah,"* says the grim-faced soldier. "Whatever, Dude," says my son with a grin. In panic I look to the floor, which will surely open up now. It doesn't. I look at the soldier. A tiny upward curve of the corners of his mouth gives way to an almost-grin. He stamps Michael's visa quickly and waves him on before a full-blown smile might break through. And I begin to remember what it's really all about. Thank you, Michael.

The next day, most of our group goes to School 15, a Moscow elementary school, to meet kids and teachers and to present a beautiful hand-made peace quilt from the children of a school in Seattle. I stay behind, waiting for Vadim and Vladimir. Vadim is a professor of philosophy at Moscow University, and Vladimir is secretary of the US/USSR Friendship Society. Both were guests in my town six months ago. We housed them and taught them to square dance and to get drunk on California wine. Now it's their turn.

They nearly crush me with their hugs, and off we go on a crazy taxi ride through crowded Moscow. I am unsure whether the ride or the cigarette smoke will get me first, but I feel so good about the genuine affection of these two Russian brothers that it doesn't matter.

At Vadim's apartment, old and small and cozy, we eat Lithuanian sausage that his mother sent; we spike the vodka with his homemade cranberry liqueur; we sing like fools, as another Vladimir, head of the Soviet Sister-city association, bangs on Vadim's old Mexican guitar. They tell jokes about Americans; I mimic the soldier at customs. Laughter fills the room, and I wonder where's the enemy? Perhaps Pogo was right!

But that's too simple. Amidst the joyful sharing, probably because of it, I begin to feel into the psyche of a people who have a very old and very different way of relating to one another, a different game-plan for survival. There is a bondedness here, a strong web or connectedness that I do not know. I like it, and I don't like it. I feel nurtured, protected by the group. And I also feel constrained. Like in a little village where the same people have lived all their lives. Everyone looks out for everyone. And everyone also makes sure that no one "colors outside the lines." Group consciousness is high; individual initiative is not valued.

In Leningrad I watched a woman walk up to a little girl, a stranger, and proceed to button her coat as if she were her own child. This is totally acceptable behavior, and it speaks of the caring and the group consciousness of Soviet society. Carried to extreme, it becomes social control. Our group visited "refusenik-families," Soviet citizens who have applied to leave the USSR and been refused. Many of them experience severe treatment, less from the government than from their own peer group, who consider them deserters of the Motherland. So much fear and yet so much love.

I have read some old Russian folk-tales which have provided a glimpse into the Russian psyche. In American folk-tales, the hero (male) rarely dies, right? In Russian tales, they (usually a group of men and women) frequently do die. A typical scenario might be that of a small town which is being attacked by some horrible enemy. The heroes and heroines block the pass while the townspeople escape to the mountains. After the townspeople are safe, the defenders fling open the gates and die gloriously in a final, futile but valiant battle.

Can you sense the difference? Not quite your typical American happy ending.

Until we learn to accept and honor the basic differences in our cultures we will never be able to work together for peace. And no one culture can do it alone. In fact, we may have co-created this planetary mess that we are in so that we can learn that very truth!

The name of the prize is not just peace. The US and the USSR have so much of value to share with one another, that we have before us not only the possibility for peaceful coexistence, but also the opportunity for a quantum leap in planetary consciousness. It's as if the US had one of the missing pieces to our shared puzzle of conscious evolution and the USSR had another. We need one another to complete the puzzle, and yet we spend most of our time and resources trying to protect our piece instead of offering it. It's so hard to admit that the "other team" might have the puzzle piece we need to complete "our" puzzle. I guess we will not be ready to complete the puzzle until we are willing to see that there is really only one team.

In Tbilisi, the capital of Georgia, I talked to a man about our planetary family, about our need to move beyond political boundaries and to recognize that we are all citizens of planet earth. He hugged me, and then he picked up a handful of dirt and held it as if it were a sacred object. He said, "Yes, I know. But do *you* know? You Americans, you have no roots. My father's father's father died to call this little piece of land home. This land is me, I am this land," he said, as he held out the dirt to me as one would hold out one's newborn child for a blessing. And I thought, "My God, there is so much I do not know." There is so much we can, must, share with one another. Roots and wings. We need to know about roots, and they need to remember their wings. They have forgotten how to fly, to soar; and we have, or at least I have, strained my connection to the sacredness of "place." Sure, anywhere I hang my hat is home, but that freedom from attachment to the place where my great-grandmother's/grandfather's bones are laid has cost me something. And hopefully, in my openness to remember, to relearn about roots from these Soviets, I make myself vulnerable to them. And in that moment, our hearts touch and we are, as I had dreamed, of one family.

When I was leaving this man, as I was turning away, he grabbed me and kissed me, no peck on the cheek, a full, on the mouth, moustache-crusher kiss that curled my socks. It was wonderful. We stood there, our eyes filling with tears and I thought, Robert Bly's "wildman" is alive and well and living in Soviet Georgia. I would give my life for that man and I was with him perhaps two hours. That is the quality of connection that is there, in the people, in the earth.

Back in my room, I got it. I understood what we must learn from one another. He can teach me how to truly love where I am. And I can help him to expand this passionate love beyond his little piece of earth. Together we can learn to love the entire planet with the fervor he feels for his Georgian soil. And then we can both, authentically, call our entire planet home, with no more boundaries and borders and ideologies over which to kill each other.

The Soviet Union is a tight, guarded society. But in the hearts of the Soviet people there are millions of "butterflies-in-potential," yearning to fly. I will return to the Soviet Union, probably soon. And again, I will find ways to move beyond the official tours and meetings and into the places where I can share my wings. And they will teach me how to touch the earth with my soul. Will you come with me?

*WWII veterans before May Day Parade, Tibilisi, Georgian Socialist Republic*

*—photo: Diana Glasgow*

# 16

# Russian Pictures

## *Winifred Rawlins*

### *Leningrad*

Here on the edge of Leningrad
in the shine of Sunday evening
after the August rain,
stroll to the Gulf of Finland
through the park with the red geraniums,
observing Railwaymen's Day.

---

Feet on the sandy pathway
move to the beat of the music
sounding the honor of railwaymen
who carry the coal and the timber
from city and forest and mine,
linking invisible arms
around the factory and field
as we link arms this evening.

---

Here on the edge of Leningrad
if you care to listen intently

along the lanes of the past,
you may hear the whine of a bomb
above the encircled city,
or else an infant's wail
whose life is flickering out
because the breast is dry.
Now on this Sunday evening
the air is warm and kind;
the children are trailing sleepily,
the music ends with a burst of praise,
the trombone player thumps the floor
and wipes his hands and brow.


# *Intourist Guide*

Little daughter of Leningrad,
lately child yet entirely woman,
your body straight like a little tree,
belying the awareness in your eyes,
from what still reservoir of control
do you draw your brief sad smiles,
your sudden delicate silences
placed like a cool veil
between us, the strangers, and your too
         responsive being?
You stand like a gallant small banner
before the shrine of your country's enigma,
which, but for your office,
you would reveal to us.
Valentina, though you valiantly defend
         your secret,
you have left your heart undefended.

# Moscow

Ah, Moscow,
you are indeed a gateway, set in both
    space and time;
you are also
he who stands at the gate and with hand
    held to his brow
gazes in both directions.

# Zagorsk

For prayer to be potent
it should be unceasing,
rising like smoke from a fire
or the perfume of flowers in May;
prayer and music interwoven
ascend from this holy place
daytime and nighttime,
filling every aperture
of the small throbbing sanctuary;
the white tongues of the candles
twinkle like stars
in the blue and red dusk,
while down from the walls
the brooding mild faces
of long-dead saints
behold the chanting monks
with brown soft hair
curling heavy on their necks.
This is a place which hears
much weeping and also rejoicing;
this place is the desired goal
of many feet traveling many roads;

these saints gaze down
on a mosaic of human forms
prostrate on the dark stone,
see many silent lips
moving in ancient syllables
while eloquent beseeching hands
invoke the power of the Cross.

On tables outside in the courtyard
where pigeons endlessly strut and coo,
small engaging wooden bears
carved at so much a dozen
for the tourist trade
see-saw impudently in the sunlight.

# *Klin*

Because you may not bring
the weather of today into this house of
        the past,
take off your shoes as you cross this
        threshold;
yet you would do no wrong
to enter so through reverence and love.
While time ran a few short paces
these walls enclosed the suffering spirit
striving to bestow on us impossible gifts
from the country of sound where he lived
        his tenderest hours.

Pyotr Ilyich*, how the ungrateful ones
placidly take your offerings hewn out of
    pain
and use them as trinkets to adorn the
    emptiness
of an idle afternoon ...
Now we who would have touched your
    hands
asking your forgiveness, bidding you
    continue
for our sake your journeys of exploration
can only greet the humble mute
    companions
of your sojourn here; for surely even they
were raised just a little from their
    common dullness
and knew they shared your destiny, your
    joy.
Your bathrobe hangs here on its wooden
    peg
above the bed so honest in its form;
it was a servant simply of your need
to regain poise and vigor for the day;
and here your desk stands in its brown
    integrity,
waiting forever for the moment of release
when you would need its strength, its
    faithful calm;
and, closest of all friends, the instrument
to whom you bared your heart now
    silently
ages and rusts, its strings from time to
    time
unwillingly vibrating at the command

(*Pyotr Ilyich Tschaikovsky)

of alien fingers. Yet, Pyotr Ilyich,
here at the end even your far-ranging
     spirit
discovered an earthly home. When the
     frost-wrapped birch trees
stood solitary in the snow
softly deep round their roots, then in the
     quietness
of the Russian winter morning your own
     deep roots
sang a new song of territories known and
     cherished,
of harbors gained. But as the long night
     approached
and new shadowy vistas opened, the wild
     wings
within you beat ever more strongly and
     urgently,
seeking an exit.


## *Kalinin*

Well, here's the ring
and we're all kids again,
spellbound by the red carpet
and the freshly spread sawdust,
the smell in our nostrils
of the rain outside
on the streets of Kalinin
and the wet folk streaming
on the little low benches,
and the fainter smell
of the urine of animals,
and the smell of excitement

in the waiting crowd;
the air fills with music
strident and hot,
and the ringmaster enters
cracking his long whip,
there's no time to breathe,
we shudder from thrill to thrill,
whirling through space
with the plump trapeze artist,
teetering on stilts
on a quivering tight-rope,
holding up a pyramid
of rubber-boned acrobats,
plunging through hoops
stuck round with knives;
now the carpet's rolled back,
there's a challenge of trumpets,
and here comes a wild horse
(My, what a beauty)
sailing over barriers
topped with fire,
throwing up the sawdust
like spray among the audience;
and suddenly, almost unnoticed, into the
        ring
comes a small absurd figure in bottle-
        green pants
hanging loose behind and long over his
        feet,
leading a donkey with a face like a gray
        sheep,
and a murmur runs along the benches—
        Karandash!
Karandash, the star of the evening, the
        great Moscow clown.
With childish futile hands

he tugs at the donkey's mouth, pointing
    to the jumps
cleared by the wild horse, and
    "immediately!" he pipes,
and "immediately!" shrills the high-
    pitched petulant voice,
while he pulls at the immobile, sheep-like
    gray mouth
and once again affection flows toward
    him from the crowd,
Karandash, the little man, the beloved of
    the people.

---

But now comes the ringmaster,
swish! flies his whip,
the red curtains part,
with a pounding of hooves
and a snorting of nostrils
and heaving of flanks,
wild horse the second,
with a bareback rider
pirouetting and cavorting
in velvet and spangles,
thunders past the benches . . .
on your shoulder falls a touch as light as
    thistledown;
you turn, and are met by brown eyes and
    a shy Russian smile;
a girl leans forward;
I, too, she whispers confidentially,
am seeing it for the first time . . .

## The Bolshoi

We who live out our lives
moving in patterns of ultimate beauty

on this vast empty stage,
speak to you, worshiping devotees
gathered under the dazzling candelabra
to pay homage and to offer us your love.
We are the priests and priestesses
of an absolute god,
total in his jealousy and his demands;
as tender children we were brought
to this temple of the dance,
and made our hesitating vows
while our young bleeding feet
strengthened and grew toward their
      rigorous destiny.
To you who have abandoned
the pious genuflection, the devout prayer,
who have bolted the doors of the golden
      churches,
we would say to you, come and learn of us
another discipline, older meditations
begun in the dim pre-history of our race,
perfected with anguish through its waking
      years.

---

A soft unearthly light
plays on the graveyard where the young
      Giselle
too early sleeps; her lover,
constant in grief and in devotion,
moves through the desolate rhythms of
      the dance.
Now the stone lifts, she rises up, she
      comes to him;
the light illumines, through the white
      impersonal dress,
her obedient body, obedient not to him

but to the ancient nuptials of her art;
now she is in his arms; now, like a cloud,
all spirit, she floats across the somber
    backdrop;
the grave opens and receives her; as she
    sinks,
the first bright shafts of the young
    morning sun
flood the great stage. Comrades, the day
    is before us!
We move toward unknown goals; the
    earlier banners
have been pulled down and trampled;
    here at the Bolshoi
we light the candles on the twin altars
of beauty and of commitment; may the
    same Power
which accepts the sacrifice of our bodies
and opens a path for the spootniks
lead us to a new God worthy of our
    praise.

## *Leaving Russia*

Here is a road
which runs out at the end
as time runs out,
without change, without reason,
but because all known things
have an ending,
the long silent road
to the western frontier,
the road to Warsaw.
The fields run past

and the birches run past
and the little log cabins
leaning into the mud,
with their blue-framed windows
cherishing geraniums,
run past as we travel;
the solitary pigs
rooting in the puddles
and the roadside cow
giving milk to a woman
and the wondering children
and small round haystacks
and ducks in the rain
run past as we travel;
and here is the ending;
suddenly they stand there,
the dark young men
with their sad strong faces
and whispered *spasebas;*
we must leave you now, fellow-voyagers
    on this ancient satellite,
our estranged brothers.
you are the only customs-men in all
    of Europe and America
who waved to us good-bye.

# 17

# US, Soviet Citizens Share Desire for Peace

## *Sharon Tennison*

On the last leg of our journey to Moscow, the fifteen of us climbed aboard a small Yugoslav plane at midnight. It was raining, the mood a bit tense, and we were exhausted. We settled in for sleep.

A tap came on my shoulder from the back. A red-haired, broad-faced woman of about 40 was smiling and asking *"Moskva, Moskva?"* "Yes, to Moscow," I replied. We began to communicate with sign language and the few words we shared in common.

Pins were exchanged, next pencils, and finally pictures. A few rows back a young Soviet woman was trying to be interpreter for several Americans and two Russians. A few more rows back food was being exchanged. The plane came alive as we flew through the night over "enemy" territory.

The camera crew for our grassroots, fact-finding delegation, asleep since takeoff, woke up to see a party in motion. The pilot was hastily consulted. Yes, the cameramen could shoot. Lights came on, cameras and booms appeared out of nowhere to capture the meeting in air of the "enemies."

The party continued and we made our descent into Moscow singing "Moscow Nights" in Russian and English. We left our new friends with hearty hugs.

The plane landed at 5 a.m. We were ushered into the black marble airport. Few lights were on, our flight friends had vanished, no one spoke English and it was ghostly quiet. Customs next—no luggage was opened. Cameras, 24 boxes of film, and 25 Americans passed without difficulty.

After settling luggage at the Cosmos tourist hotel, we were shown the subway and were free to use it as we chose. It took courage the first time, but as the Cyrillic alphabet became a bit more familiar, maps were consulted and we got braver. We took our own interpreter, but she could not go in 20 directions at one time. Numbers of Russians came to our rescue as we stood confused at intersections.

Our official tour guide from Intourist took us to see the museums and city highlights. Our joggers were out on the streets early. We traveled in groups of two to five people going in different directions. There was no sense of being followed, and Russians didn't seem to have any fear in stopping us to practice English.

Through official channels we arranged to talk with the Peace Committee, Friendship Society, and the Women's Committee. We also visited several schools, pioneer palaces, a factory, a hospital of our choice (we asked a nurse for a typical hospital and requested to go there) and worshiped in a vital Baptist Church that was packed on a Tuesday evening.

Unofficially, we ate dinner in apartments, had coffee with Soviets in small restaurants, met people in parks, were invited to a wedding reception (much like our own), visited dissidents, danced in nightclubs, and left town on an old commuter bus. We visited a firehouse, private produce market, Russian Orthodox service, and a Catholic mass. Photos with names and addresses were exchanged.

There were two skirmishes with the KGB—once when we invited a college student to dinner at our hotel and he was wisked away to a fate unknown, and when one of our photographers was photographing people in line for consumer goods. Our peace button saved the day for the film. When he flashed the friendship message on the button, they apologized and released him.

Soviet apartments are small, plain, and utilitarian. They resemble some of our government housing with one exception—we saw no litter, graffiti, or evidence of abuse. As others traveling in the Soviet Union have noted, people walk in the streets at all hours of the night without concern. One Soviet woman attributed the safe streets to the lack of violence allowed on TV. She was aware of American TV and cinema and connected this to street crime. We did check Russian TV; a soccer game was the most violent program.

We experienced the controlled society. Russians feel it is easing up year by year. In an apartment for dinner, we were told, "I couldn't have had you here 10 years ago, five years ago it would have been questionable, but today it is OK."

Ileya Orlov, minister of the Moscow Baptist Church since 1946, spoke of lessening tensions in relation to religion. Later we heard a fiery sermon in Baptist tradition from the Moscow pulpit. Coming from a Baptist background, I enjoyed hearing the hymns of childhood sung in another language.

Most of the people we talked with believe in their system, see it needing improvements, but on the whole working fairly well for them. It is not working in our terms because they are short of consumer goods and their standard of living is well below ours.

Official people openly talked of wishing their homes were large enough to accommodate foreigners overnight, but local people who had us in seemed unaware of their limited space. It was the visit and friendship that mattered. I was reminded of my parents' standard of living when I was a child. It was poor contrasted with mine now, yet they and their neighbors felt grateful for what they had—this was the feeling I gleaned from the Soviets.

In short, we experienced a good cross-section of Soviet life. We came away with many preconceived stereotypes demolished and feeling that we must lower the walls of misinformation, condemnation, and hatred. We met no barbarians, no "people with little respect for life," only generous people who are preoccupied with talking about peace and petrified of war.

The last Russian I saw was a burly, red-faced man in military uniform on the train as we left Leningrad. Attempts to talk with him were unsuccessful. I finally pulled my friendship button out and touched his lapel in an act of giving it to him to wear. He was exasperated with me, but looked closer at the wording on the pin. I saw his eyes light up, and the next second I was wrapped up in a big hug and had a kiss planted firmly on my cheek. We couldn't speak each other's language, but we had communicated about our common concern for friendship and peace. He put the pin in his pocket, said "spaceba" (thank you) and scurried off to his official business.

# 18

# To Live
# Without Enemies

*Gene Knudsen-Hoffman*

On a warm, sunny September day in 1983, I walked into a building in Moscow that was surrounded with gardens and trees. I was led into a cool, dark room with big windows, where I sat alone and waited. Soon a woman with soft blonde hair and a gentle, yearning face came to greet me, carrying a gift: a recording of one of Tschaikovsky's masses.

Nina Bobrova and I had met the previous spring at a Soviet Peace Committee meeting. She was the representative of the External Relations Department of the Metropolitan Filaret of Byelorussia and Minsk, who is known for his keen interest in peace. I was representing the Fellowship of Reconciliation's US-USSR Reconciliation Program. We talked of our longing for peace between our two nations, of our coming to know one another's people. "Could you," Nina asked "bring together Russian religious women with American religious women in the United States?" "I don't know," I responded. "But I will try."

Four months later arrangements were under way. Don George, Director of La Casa de Maria, an Immaculate Heart retreat center in Santa Barbara, California, offered their beautiful facilities for the retreat at no cost. The national office of the Fellowship of Reconciliation agreed to organize a national tour for the women. The Resource Center for Nonviolence in Santa Cruz would organize a California tour. We began to select fifteen American participants.

One year later, on January 28, flower-laden members of Santa Barbara's FOR Chapter met the four Soviet women at the Santa Barbara airport and took them in triumph to their retreat home for four days. The American participants from across the US had been selected for their lives of commitment and peace activity. Denominations represented included Presbyterian, Roman Catholic, Quaker, Reform Jewish, United Church of Christ, Mennonite, Lutheran, Buddhist, and Russian Orthodox. Ages ranged from twenty to somewhere in the seventies.

As retreat leader, I used the discussion guide I'd created for our US-USSR program, "Learning to Love the Stranger," and a Quaker process called Creative Listening. Its purpose is to engage in dialogue with the question and to listen carefully to one another's responses without answering or challenging them.

In our first sessions we explored our childhoods and our significant spiritual experiences.

Nina Bobrova, who led the Soviet delegation, was born in Japan to a Russian family. Her first language was Japanese. Her family was very religious, but her school friends were Japanese Buddhists; thus she learned ecumenism early. She went to the Soviet Union when she was twenty-two.

Tatiana Volgina, born in Moscow in 1943, lived in a huge house with other families and loved the open-door neighborliness of it. Her family was also very religious. She works in the editorial department of the Moscow Patriarchate.

Tatiana (Tanya) Novikova, the youngest member of the delegation works in the ecumenical department of the Patriarchate. Her father is a priest of the Orthodox Church.

Mother Marfa Kovalevich, a nun from a village in Byelorussia, was born in an animal shed at the height of World War II. The family home and barn had burned to the ground. Her parents were very religious and her happiest memory was the "fairy tree" at Christmas, decorated with toys made from paper.

The Americans, all of them peace activists, included a rabbi with a congregation in Albuquerque, a black peace and civil rights leader from Harlem, a minister in the Lutheran Church of Santa Barbara, teachers, community leaders, Catholic sisters and a university student.

Religious experiences among the Americans were varied. One had a period of deep wrestling to determine she had gifts equal to men and that God transcended male clergy! (She was not alone in this.) Another was startled into a life of spirituality by Dietrich Bonhoeffer's words: "Act and then belief will come." Another's transformation came when she took severe personal risks to help integrate a black school. One person found her spiritual life through living for eight years with a diagnosis of terminal cancer and a death experience. Another found it alone in a tiny room in New York where she was studying to become an actress. She described how the room became radiant as she feverishly wrote a poem about her life as a journey into God. One woman's turning came at a Mennonite college where she heard the Bible she had rejected transformed by new interpretations. Illness, injustice, the pain of discrimination or just early training were some of the promptings that turned these women toward a life of the spirit.

Among the Soviet women, three were raised in the Eastern Orthodox tradition from birth and did not have the struggles of the Americans. Only Nina Bobrova, who was born in Japan, was exposed to another religion: Buddhism. She came to her life work for peace and the Orthodox Church through a Japanese Orthodox priest.

In each session we addressed different questions: Have you felt a spiritual power in your life that Gandhi declared had the energy equal to the force of an atom bomb? Can you describe a way you have invited goodness from a person who has harmed you? How might you express concern for an oppressor when you work for justice?

Describe a way you might live to reduce the pain of others; a way your nation could do the same. One afternoon we explored what brought us joy, pain, anxiety, and hope. And finally, how we and the Soviets might save one another's lives. The most fruitful question was the one that exposed our differences, separated us in anger and tears and brought some healing.

Even though we recognized that the Soviet women had to speak from within the framework of the religious and political policies of their government, it was hard, if not impossible for us to accept that. There was some relief when we recognized similar attitudes among ourselves. One Catholic Sister remarked, "They're just like we were before Vatican II. We knew the shortcomings of our orders, the errors, even the corruptions, but we were so imbued with an idea of loyalty that we would only whisper about them among ourselves. To the outside world, we presented the face of unity, if not of love." Here are some actual conversations we transcribed.

*Kathy:* I see the sanctuary movement as breaking a chain of violence in America, and actually saving lives. It is inspiring that some of us are willing to take great risks to save lives of people our government would send back to their countries to be killed. Another is bringing people here so we can actually understand what is going on in other parts of the world and thus change our misperceptions.

*Tatiana:* I think maybe there is no fear of Americans in the Soviet Union, only of weapons. To break the chain of these fears, I think we must learn more about each other. We must speak about common things first, things which do not divide us, but can join us together. Perhaps after we learn, we know, we understand, we can speak about things that separate us.

*Gene:* I feel I could break a chain by looking for things in my nation and my government I can affirm. I feel there is so much in my culture I fear and disapprove of that I've lost my love for things American. If I can keep seeking the good in my country and my people and share these discoveries with others, a chain of violence, fear and injustice in me would be broken.

*Nina:* There's not enough knowledge about each other. We want to give you more information about the reality of our life. Very little is known of our idea of peace and beauty and our work for it. So I think it is important to know what we are doing, and how we can unite ourselves to do what you call the peace strike. Another thing: we don't talk about the "enemy." We talk about the militaristic tendencies of your government: we do not consider your people as enemies. But in America, you put us all together as Soviets and you are against us. The word "communism" is a fearful word here. You forget that not all of us are communists and those who are are also human beings.

*Fran:* I've had a kind of secret here and I've been trying to cover it up. About a year ago I was on India Airlines and when they said, "Now you're traveling over Moscow," I felt afraid. I'm a peace activist and I'm supposed to have all the right feelings. I was shocked to find that I felt afraid.

I was raised in a conservative place in the 50s, when communism and the punishment of communism were very dominant. Even at that time, I thought I was kind of crazy. But only once before have I ever met a Russian in my whole life. I can accept philosophically that we should be friends; I can even accept it practically. But when it comes down to speaking my truth to you, I'm afraid. I mean, we really have to be honest about our feelings with each other even if it doesn't make us look so glorious. There are a lot of differences I don't understand and I think we're afraid to question very deeply because there's so much at risk. And a friendship that has as much to risk as our friendship is very difficult even to begin—and that makes me afraid, too. And I'm crying about that . . .

*Beverly:* As long as Fran is willing to share her secrets, I want to share mine. And I say this with, hopefully, humility. I feel we're vulnerable. I think that Nina wants to speak only of the positive and begin our friendship there. I do too. (In tears.) There is much to repent of in my country. You've told me that, and I want to. But isn't there repentance in your country? It seems to me it's dishonest to come to each other speaking only of the wonderful things we have in common. There is terrible injustice in my country against your country, and I hate that. But there must be things, too, in your world—and we have to come with equal hands. It's not all *my* culture, *my* guilt; that's a heavy load for me to bear.

*Gene:* I think there's something we're not dealing with: that we are each dangerous to the other. Your weapons are as dangerous to us as our weapons to you. And if you can acknowledge that you are dangerous to us, I think it would be a truth our friendship could begin with.

*Nina:* The weapons, wherever they are, are dangerous. They are for killing. But actually, our country has been all the time trying to make initiatives for peace and we Russian people are afraid of war, much more than you. We know what war is. None of you has gone through being under siege by the Nazis; none of you has had to dig a hole in the ground and live there. That is why our country is afraid. Twenty million of us were killed, and more than that were homeless. In 1946 my country said immediately we must get rid of all armaments. So I just can't sit here with these big differences of understanding. Please don't call us enemies.

*Margaret Rose:* I think we have two things in common right here. We are all children of God and we're all women. I really believe that the major problems are the political systems in both our countries. I honestly think it's sort of "old boys" system. It's a male, hierarchical one that has kept women silent. And that's what I'd like to see us begin to talk about. I'd like to see us explore ways the women of the world could set up a new model.

*Anne:* What I see is that from both sides there has been a negative influence on the third world. But I believe we can both cooperate to have a positive influence. Some of the best inroads toward US-USSR reconciliation can be made on common ground: fighting disease, fighting hunger, which are enemies of the whole world. If we use the gifts of technology, the gifts of education that our countries have to help the rest of the world, then maybe something can be done between *us.*

*Mary Evelyn:* I thank Nina for helping me experience and understand the reality of the terrible suffering in World War II. The task for us is to realize that what you described and what you suffered can never be repeated because that kind of war cannot be fought.

*Mariquita:* There is a Buddhist practice: if you feel anger and aggression against someone, give that person a gift. You cannot continue to feel the anger and aggression while you're thinking about giving a gift. What gifts can we give each other?

And so the retreat ended. I've only been able to give you a taste of what happened; there was much more. We discussed the question of whether believers could be in high government positions in the Soviet Union. The answer was no. We discussed, with frustration, the status of Jews in the Soviet Union. We drafted a statement. We honored one another by worshiping in the different modes we represented. We recognized that to begin any friendship we'd better study one another's histories.

Some of us left the retreat satisfied that we had made some small beginnings; many of us did not get our questions answered. But all of us tried to listen in love and keep open to one another and I think we did that.

They agreed to ask both governments to negotiate toward disarmament, to discontinue testing and production of all chemical, biological, laser and nuclear weapons, and to halt the arms race and the militarization of space.

Two ideas emerged for our US-USSR Reconciliation Program. One is that the FOR initiate a nationwide, week-long US-USSR teach-in and that we invite the Soviets to initiate a USSR-US teach-in at the same time. We would encourage every peace center and every school, every college, every university in the country to join in it. Each community would use whatever resources it has.

The second is to cooperate in areas where both our nations agree we have problems. For example, the Soviets admit they have problems of alcoholism and a high divorce rate. So do we. We could pool our knowledge and wisdom on these two subjects.

In this way we would be giving gifts to one another, relating as equals, and exploring both our differences and our common ground. In this way, too, we would begin to answer Abraham Lincoln's question: "Do I not destroy my enemies when I make them my friends?"

*MARINA*
*Confection worker,*
*Moscow*

# 19

# Two Faces
# of Mother Russia

*Jean Lewis-Snable*

> Life has always seemed to me like a plant that lives
> on its rhizome. Its true life is invisible, hidden in the
> rhizome. The part that appears above ground lasts
> only a single summer. Then it withers away—an
> ephemeral apparition. When we think of the unend-
> ing growth and decay of life and civilizations, we
> cannot escape the impression of absolute nullity. Yet
> I have never lost a sense of something that lives and
> endures underneath the eternal flux. What we see is
> the blossom, which passes. The rhizome remains.

This passage from Carl Jung's *Memories, Dreams, Reflections*
describes my experience at the Mamayev Hill Memorial at
Volgograd. As our Volga River boat approached the city of
Volgograd, we saw the statue of a woman rising from the
highest hill on the horizon. Our guide told us that this is the
largest free-standing statue in the world and it depicts the
Motherland calling upon her sons to rise to her defense and
"rid the world of violence." Many people on the boat were
carrying flowers. They were making a pilgrimage to this
"sacred" place and would place the flowers at the
memorial. I picked up a red rose that had fallen on the deck
of the boat, and carried it with me as we left the river and
continued our journey toward the Memorial site.

Mamayev Hill, the highest point of the city that had been known as Stalingrad, had been the front line of the battle to save the city from German invasion during World War II. The city, now known as Volgograd, has constructed a memorial complex on the summit of this hill as a tribute to those who died defending their city.

Tiers of stairs lead up to the commanding figure of Mother Russia. Brandishing a sword in her right hand, and looking back, she urges her defenders on with her outstretched left hand. Her mouth is wide open in a war cry, as she calls her sons to join in her defense.

The groups of stairs lead on through an alley of tall poplar trees which converge on a huge sculpture "Stand to the Death"—the figure of a soldier clutching a grenade in his right hand and carrying a machine gun in his left hand. He rises from a rock in the midst of a reflecting pool of water. Beyond him, stairs lead between demolished walls symbolizing the ruined walls of Stalingrad, and carrying slogans that had been seen in many parts of the city during the fighting. "Not a step back" and "Beyond the Volga is no place for us" are reminders of the battles that raged from November 1942 to February 1943.

We pass by other figures of battle scenes, and then the stairs lead us into an underground opening below the base of the "Motherland" statue. We move down into a rotunda, "The Hall of Military Glory," which had been dug into the earth and lined with wall mosaics that bear the names of those soldiers who were killed in action. These names cover the full length of the hall. The music of Schumann's "Traumerei" is played over and over again as "pilgrims" move from one mosaic panel to the next. In the center of the hall a huge marble hand, many stories tall, extends from the earth and holds a gigantic torch of the Eternal Flame. It is at the base of this emerging hand that the people lay their flower offerings. Tears were sliding down the cheeks of many of those who, silently and with eyes closed, placed their flowers before the Eternal Flame. I sensed a mood of worshipful adoration and quiet awe, as I, too, offered a flower—the rose I had taken from the boat deck—in silent communion with the pilgrims in a spirit of peace.

The women, men, and children continued around the rotunda, stopping at certain places, as if they had read the name of someone they had known. I felt an emotional binding together, too deep to find expression in any of the outside world's languages.

We filed outside into the naturally sunlit atmosphere. Before us there appears another statue. This is very different from the imposing Motherland urging her sons with a drawn sword, hand gesture, and battlecry. Wordlessly, people pass by this figure. This is also the figure of a woman. To me it speaks from a different side of Mother Russia. This woman is seated, shrouded in a hooded grieving-veil. Although her face is shadowed by the veil, her eyes are cast down upon the draped body of her dead son which is resting over her lap. Her body seems to be part of the earth itself. The image of Michelangelo's "Pieta" came into my consciousness as I felt pulled by a power beyond myself. I was drawn by a magnetic eternal mother grieving over her sacrificed son. This feeling of the universal mother's experience of the pain of war touched on a suffering so deep that it is beyond sound itself.

I found myself wondering if the sculptor had consciously imitated the "Pieta" as a means of catharsis, or if the artist was responding to the rhizome within himself, the rhizome which expresses the eternal love of the grieving mother. Those of us who felt the strange power of this statue seemed to me to be experiencing the heartache of the soul of all mothers whose sons' lives had been sacrificed for her preservation, the life of the Motherland. We were invisibly bound together in a communion beyond that which our conscious minds could express.

The sharing of this feeling ties into Jung's description of the rhizome. I, an American woman, connected with Russian women on a deep emotional level beyond verbal expression. It seemed as if we were in touch with a part of ourselves that spread as an underground connection which surfaces wherever the grieving mother takes back the body of her sacrificed son.

Are there two faces of Mother Russia? Is one calling her children to battle to save her, the Motherland? Is the other the woman whose love embraces the sacrificed and through her grief pleads for an end to war?

*Mother weeping over fallen son, Mamayev Hill Memorial, Volgograd*

# 20

# It's Warm in Siberia

## *Jon Humboldt Gates*

A ten-foot rooster tail of spray shot up from the stern of the speeding hydrofoil, a rainbow arcing in its fine mist. The Siberian sun warmed the air as our ferry skimmed along the placid waters of the mile-wide Angara River. Russian passengers chatted with one another and stood at the railings of the craft to view the rugged wilderness of the river valley and the mountains beyond.

The public pier had been jammed with people that morning. The stores and factories of the nearby city of Irkutsk had been closed in observance of a Soviet national holiday. I had stood for more than two hours to buy my ticket, and from my place in line, had seen the tourist boat arrive, load its passengers, and depart without delay—no lines, no wait, and no Russian passengers.

I felt happier to be sitting in the stern of the public hydrofoil, surrounded by local sightseers. A few of them appeared to be dressed for a stroll in the tropics, wearing colorful short-sleeved sun shirts, dark glasses, sandals, and carrying cameras. Wasn't this Siberia? Land of frozen exiles?

An hour after departing Roketa Public Pier near Irkutsk, our hydrofoil slowed and lowered its hull into the icy waters of Baikal, the largest freshwater lake in the world. Within minutes, the sleek ferry was moored to the dock, and a metal gangway lowered to its deck. Passengers slowly disembarked from the craft, walking in both directions along a narrow paved road which skirted a portion of the lake's western shore.

The day was hot. After walking about a mile along the asphalt road, I stopped, took off my coat, and sat on a large outcropping of rock. I could see only the southern tip of the 450-mile-long lake. A faint haze hung in the air, turning the tall mountains on the far eastern shore into a mysterious purple escarpment hovering above the water's surface. The surrealism of this panorama cast my senses into a timeless daydream.

This was only my fourth day on Russian soil. The previous days had been spent aboard the Trans-Siberian Express, and, during that train ride, my comprehension of the Russian language had been put into its true perspective—I knew very little. Struggling with the Russians' non-textbook phrasing, and my limited vocabulary, had proven as stressful as chopping knotted firewood with a dull axe.

A loud splash snapped my attention in the opposite direction. Beneath the near freezing waters of Baikal, I saw the milky-white form of a swimmer. His head burst to the surface with a primal scream and he thrashed about madly to keep his muscles and joints from seizing in the cold. He paused for a moment to tread water and look back to shore, noticing me for the first time. He gave a yell in Russian, "Come swimming, for your health!"

I knew how invigorating the frigid mountain lake would feel, but I only waved and smiled. A minute later his pestering voice shouted, "Hey, come here!" He had returned to shore and was drying himself while madly motioning me to come and talk with him. I felt annoyed at his persistence, and tried to wave him away, but he wouldn't give up. The swimmer struggled to pull his pants on while making his way toward me on the beach. Damn! Halfheartedly I stood up and walked down to see what he wanted.

"You are a foreigner? Yes?" He eagerly thrust out his cold hand to shake mine. His handshake was electrified from the lake swim.

The swimmer talked so rapidly that my limited Russian was pushed beyond understanding. I looked at him and guessed that he was about 35. He was short in stature, almost elfin, with twinkling eyes, large ears, a grin across his face, and gesticulating hands that tried to describe what I might miss from his vigorous speech. My apprehensions suddenly disappeared. I liked this man.

"Yes, I'm a foreigner. I'm from the USA."

"Amerikanets!" he exclaimed, pumping my arm vigorously. "Good to meet you. Very good." He again flew into a friendly tirade of words. At best, I was on the outer perimeters of deciphering his rapid-fire speech, but I nodded eagerly, laughed, and looked at his eyes.

"Where's your group?" he asked. "What, no group? You're alone? Very good! An American traveler alone in Russia! And you speak Russian." His excitement grew. Then suddenly, a serious expression froze his face. He grabbed my elbow. "You are the first American I have met. But do not be afraid. I am not a communist!"

I burst out laughing at such a statement. He shot me an inquisitive look, then returned to his fervent manner, grabbed my hand again, and introduced himself as Anatoly. I asked him to speak more slowly. He tried, but his runaway energy resembled a wild horse biting a restraining bit. While putting on his shirt and shoes he carried on two simultaneous conversations, one describing the natural wonders of Lake Baikal, the other about a school he attended in Irkutsk.

Anatoly stopped his orations abruptly, pointed into the hills, and said, "Jon! Come to my house. Please, be my guest." He grabbed my arm with one hand, picked up his towel and bag with the other, and urged me along the path.

When I decided to accompany him, he was delighted. His ravings took on a new excitement. A brief moment of self-doubt surfaced when I wondered if Anatoly was a Russian lunatic. But as we walked together, I became quite comfortable with his sincerity. He managed to speak more slowly and simply, although his intensity remained.

We walked through the village of Listvanka and followed a rutted dirt road up into the hills far above the lake. The steepness and greenery of the landscape reminded me of the inland hills of Northern California, and, for a brief moment, I entertained the notion that this was Humboldt County. The roughly fenced yards and little wooden homes along the dirt road could easily be the backwood neighborhoods of Orleans, Briceland, or Westhaven. With Anatoly at my side though, it was impossible to stray far from the fact that this was Russia. I was curious to see where we were going.

Along the road we met two young country school girls who, with one glance at my silver and black, ultra-light, hi-tech hiking shoes, knew that I was not a local. They chattered between themselves while stealing shy glances. Anatoly said something funny to them that made them dart away with embarrassed laughter.

About 200 feet ahead of us, a large older woman in a floral print dress stood stout-legged in front of the gate to a small house. With her hands resting on each hip, she resembled a vase with two handles. She waved and quickly disappeared behind a high wooden fence. "That's my mother," Anatoly said, as we neared the house where she had been standing.

Before following him through the gate, I stopped and looked back down the little valley to the peak-roofed homes of Listvanka, and beyond to Lake Baikal. The noon sun flooded the valley, a breeze rustled the trees and hillside grasses, and a large shrub hung over the wooden fence, radiating a brilliant display of pink blossoms. This was a Siberia I had never considered.

Anatoly popped his head through the gate to see where I was and told me that a lunch was being prepared. We walked along a wooden path that led to the front door of an oddly-shaped little weathered blue house with white peeling trim. I ducked my head to enter the low doorway and was greeted by the sight of a lopsided pantry room which tested my sense of equilibrium. The floor was tilted, the ceiling slanted, and trapezoidal window frames appeared to float lazily in the walls. I seriously doubted that a plumb bob or level had been consulted in the construction of this room.

Anatoly grinned and jerked his head with a motion to follow him into the next room. The unmistakable aroma of fresh bread was accented by the mustiness of old furniture and wallpaper. I noticed that the rest of the house construction followed the more conventional parallel and perpendicular lines. When we entered the kitchen, Anatoly's mother was standing with her back to us at the woodburning cookstove preparing a hot lunch. She turned for a moment to greet me with a warm smile and a hello before resuming her work. She was slicing hot bread.

An older man had been relaxing at the kitchen table with a cigarette in hand, staring out a paned window into the vegetable and flower garden. He appeared to be in his mid-seventies. His facial characteristics looked as if they had been chiseled from the birch tree of Russian history—long deep lines, a strong bone structure, and firmly entrenched eyes that reflected not so much the moment, but a deep inner brooding. Anatoly introduced me to his father. The man stood up, said hello in a gravelly voice, shook my hand, and offered me a chair at the table next to him. His name was Anton.

I set my shoulder bag in a kitchen corner on the cracked linoleum floor. Anatoly bustled around, hanging up our coats, clearing off the table, and telling his parents that I was an American from California. He explained how we had met. During this brief account, Anton listened and nodded approvingly from behind his cigarette. Anatoly's mother, Galina, kept walking between the stove and the table, delivering plates and bowls filled with food, and making sure that I was comfortable. In a matter of moments the table was covered with an enormous dinner.

Anton lifted the lid from a large yellow bowl and slowly enunciated the word for its contents. "Pir-osh-ki." He accented each syllable. "Very good to eat."

"I know about piroshki," I replied. "What kind are they?"

Anton grinned and looked at Galina and Anatoly. "This American knows about Russian food," he joked. "Yes?" He turned back to me. "Mushroom and cabbage. Do you know these other things?" He motioned to the various food dishes covering the table.

My Russian language ability was limited, but food was a topic I knew. With a small ray of confidence I scanned the table. The homemade bread was still warm and closest to me. I pointed to it. *"Xleb."* A plate of garden tomatoes and cucumber, *"pomidor e oguretz."* A bowl of sour cream, *"semetana."* The cabbage soup, *"shchi."* The cheese, *"sear."* Butter, *"maslo,"* . . . until I came to the last plate. Fish, *"reeba."* I had passed the test. Anatoly slapped my shoulder. Galina's round face broke into a quiet laughter. She insisted that we eat right away before the dinner got cold, but Anton interrupted her.

"Wait. You are the first American to come to our house. You speak to us in Russian, and you know all of our food." His hand again made a sweeping gesture at the table. "And today is a holiday. First, a drink."

Anton snapped his index finger to his throat, a Russian gesture which indicates the intent to share a drink. He rustled around in a cupboard behind his chair and came up with a bottle of dry red wine from the Georgian Republic. Anatoly found a corkscrew, opened the bottle, and filled three water glasses. Galina abstained from the alcohol.

Anton picked up his glass. With a resolute voice he toasted to health, *"na zdarovuya!"* Anatoly and I, holding our glasses up, repeated the phrase. I put the glass to my nose, and from the practiced technique of California wine tasting, sniffed the aroma, swirled the wine to release its bouquet, and washed a small sip over my tongue for taste.

Suddenly, I was aware that Anatoly and his father were both watching me anxiously. Their empty glasses were already on the table. This, I realized, was not the

Mendocino Valley wine country. This was Siberia. I tilted the glass back to my lips and gulped down the Georgian red, then set the glass on the table with theirs. They looked relieved. My spiraling perceptions were thankful that it had not been vodka.

When we started lunch, Galina hovered over my plate like a watchful owl, prodding me to try more piroshki, more fish, more soup, another cup of tea. She was obviously a conspirator from that relentless world-wide group that hold vigils over its sons and guests—The International Motherhood of Full Plates.

When I thought I could eat no more, Galina brought in three large bowls with different types of wild berries in each, a plate of cookies, and another pot of black tea. Anton picked up a cookie and dipped it in his tea.

"Many of the days I see foreigners at the lake," he said, "They walk in their groups and talk their own languages. Mostly Europeans and Japanese, a few Americans. But you are the first foreigner to come to my house."

Across the table from where I sat, the multi-paned window looked out onto a flower garden abundant with pink cosmos and colorful sweetpeas. The entire garden was in bloom. While eating a bowl of blackberries and sour cream, my mind wandered through the garden and down the valley to the lake.

"Lake Baikal contains 20 percent of the world's fresh water supply . . . it has 80 unique species of plants and animals . . . visibility underwater is 180 feet . . . there are 360 rivers and streams that feed it . . ." My mind quickly returned to the warm sunlit kitchen, the home cooking, and the Russian hospitality that surrounded me.

I sipped my tea and looked over at Anatoly, noticing an old black and white photograph hanging crookedly on the wall behind his head. The framed image was of Russian soldiers. Stalin stood in their midst.

"You are looking at this photograph?" Anatoly asked, wheeling around in his chair and pointing. Before I could comment, he interjected, "That's my father." He stood up and pressed his finger to the glass showing me a young officer with an arched back. The soldier's boyish face was smooth looking. I glanced over at Anton, he appeared not to be listening. The garden view held his interest. His mind was elsewhere.

Anatoly continued. "I told you that I am not a communist, but my father is a communist. He was in the army when he was younger. World War II was a very hard time in Russia." Anatoly's eyes widened when he said these last words. I understood the emphasis. Anton's surviving four years of war on the Russian-German front as a field officer had probably been comparable to a journey through Dante's *Inferno*.

War, with its reptillian undercurrents, and unrefereed battlefields, had undoubtedly put many of those deep lines in Anton's face. I looked back to him. He sat motionless, a slow tumbling cloud of smoke rising from his cigarette. Images of horror crept up in my mind—the siege of Leningrad, one million dead, the defense of Stalingrad, more than a million lives lost in bitter street fighting during the winter. Those realities seemed a long way from the warm, quiet little Siberian cottage where we sat that afternoon. I wanted to say something meaningful to Anton, but managed only a mundane question about how he liked Lake Baikal. He was silent for a moment, then replied that he most enjoyed resting and being near the lake. He nodded his head slowly and added, "Here, at Lake Baikal, it is very quiet."

After finishing the tea and berries Anatoly invited me to see the rest of the house. Galina already had cleared the dishes away and was sitting outside in the afternoon sun cleaning mushrooms. Their house was small; a pantry, the large open-rafter kitchen and sitting area, a sardine-can living room with a seven-foot ceiling, and a second story bedroom with four big windows facing down the valley. Anatoly led the way up a back staircase to the second story bedroom.

On the stairs I glanced at my watch and realized that the last ferry to Irkutsk was leaving in 20 minutes. Until this moment, time had seemed a remote concern. A minor panic arose. Baikal Pier was three miles away. I told Anatoly my concern. He didn't flinch, but sat down on one of the three beds in the room. "No need to worry," he reassured me, waving his hand in a casual sweep. "No problem." I was somewhat relieved, but waited judiciously to hear the solution.

"I too must go to Irkutsk tonight. I have a bus ticket, and I will take you on the bus with me." Anatoly told me that the next bus wouldn't leave for another two hours. My panic retreated.

In one corner of the bedroom I spotted a balalaika leaning against a wall. This wooden triangular-bodied, three-stringed instrument is as much a part of Russian culture as babushkas and borshch. I asked Anatoly if I could play it. "Do you play the balalaika?" he chimed. I told him no, but that I played a guitar.

My fingers strummed the oddly tuned instrument. The music for the film *Doctor Zhivago* came to my mind. I plunked out a melody on the high string and found a simple pattern that kept the other two strings harmonious. My bludgeoning technique made the instrument sound more like a banjo.

Anatoly grabbed my arm. "Come! I want you to play for my mother." He led me by the arm downstairs, through the lopsided pantry room, and out into the fenced-in garden. Galina was sitting over a high tub of freshly gathered mushrooms, cleaning and preparing them to preserve for the winter. "Mother, listen!" Anatoly burst out. "Jon plays the balalaika!" He earnestly found a seat for me on the porch, then proudly stepped back as if unveiling a new discovery.

I sat the instrument across my left knee and plunked away for several minutes, producing what sounded like an American folk melody. Galina and Anatoly listened. When I was done, they politely gave me a backyard applause. Anatoly told me that his mother also played the balalaika.

"Then you must play for me," I told her, and handed the vintage wooden instrument over to her. She first wiped her hands dry on her apron before taking it. Galina held the balalaika like a dear friend, adjusted the tuning pegs, and strummed a traditional Russian song which brought the instrument's authentic sound to life. She began playing slowly, then spontaneously increased the tempo with vigor until her right hand was a blur of sixteenth notes. The melody was a blend of folk simplicity, with a hint of oriental mystery.

This moment of music touched me deeply. As I sat and listened to Galina play the balalaika—the tub of mushrooms at her feet, Anatoly sitting next to me on the front step, the afternoon dinner behind us, the wine, the uncontrived simple conversations, Anton's brooding but hospitable nature, their small cottage, the dirt country road, the nearby village of Listvanka, Baikal, Siberia—I felt that I was touching the heart of Russia. Only then did I begin to understand a word I had learned in the Russian language which is not easily translated into English and difficult for a foreign mind to fathom. It describes the Russians' deep-rooted affinity for the land on which they have lived for more than a millenium. The word is *Kodina*—the motherland.

With a grin of satisfaction, Galina struck a resounding chord that finished her song. She looked over to me.

"Tell me, Galina," I said, "Where did you learn to play music? You play so well."

She gently set the balalaika down in the grass, leaning its fretted neck against the house. "When I was six years old I was given a balalaika." She reached into the tub of water and took out a large orange mushroom. "I learned to play by ear and from friends."

"That's how I learned," I replied. "No school, only in life."

She laughed, nodding at my remark. "That's very good to learn. Music and life."

Anatoly had momentarily disappeared, but soon returned with two large glasses of kvas, a Russian drink made from whole wheat bread fermented in water. When he told me it was kvas my stomach took a turn. Two days before I had stopped on an Irkutsk street corner after noticing several people with their noses to the sky, drinking an amber liquid that looked like apple juice. I purchased a tall mugful of the substance, which the vendor dipped from a 100-gallon kvas tank on wheels, and drank it down. The first gulp was shocking. There is nothing in America that resembles kvas. Its taste lingers questionably between a stale cider and sourdough bread. After that first streetside encounter, I vowed it would never pass my lips again.

Standing before Anatoly, I humbly thanked him for the tall glass of kvas and looked down at the small particles of soggy brown bread floating in murky water. He lifted his glass. "To health!" I wasn't so sure.

"To friendship!" I replied.

It tasted wonderful! I told him that it was much better than the street vendor's. He wrinkled his face at the notion of a vendor's kvas, and pointed to his mother confidently. "She makes the best kvas."

Anton came out of the house to join us in the garden. Anatoly took the empty glasses back in and quickly returned with his small bag of books and clothes. He pointed to my watch and said that we should start walking for Listvanka to meet the bus.

Galina set her mushrooms aside and handed Anatoly a large cloth bag filled with dozens of piroshkis, fresh cucumbers and tomatoes, cookies and a container of berries. She kissed him goodbye on the cheek. Anton stood up, gripped my hand in a firm acknowledgment of our meeting, and wished me good fortune on my travels in Russia. He then sat down near a bush of sweetpeas and lit another cigarette.

I turned to Galina. She reached out both hands to me and held mine for a moment. She smiled and simply said, "Thank you for coming to our home. Goodbye."

"A big thanks to you," I said, and then added, "To life and music!"

"Yes. To life and music," she repeated happily.

Anatoly held the gate open for me, and the next moment we were walking side by side down the dirt road toward Lake Baikal. In a matter of hours we would be back in the city of Irkutsk. We stopped for a few moments to feel the last rays of sunlight. My frozen images of Siberia melted in its warmth.

*PETER*
*Architect,*
*Moscow*

# Selected Bibliography

Arbatov, George. *The Soviet Viewpoint.* New York: Dodd,
    Mead & Co., 1981.
Barnett, Richard. *The Giants.* New York: Simon & Shuster,
    1977.
Brown, Dale W., Editor. *What About the Russians?* Elgin,
    IL: Brethren Press, 1984.
Dostoyevsky, Fyodor. *The Brothers Karamazov.* New York:
    The New American Library, 1957.
Fothergill, Dorothy. *Russia and Her People.* Moscow: Pro-
    gress Publishers, 1982.
Halliday, Fred. *Soviet Policy in the Arc of Crisis.* Washington:
    Institute for Policy Studies, 1981.
Higginbotham, Jay. *Fast Train Russia.* New York: Dodd,
    Mead, & Co., 1983.
Mamonova, Tatyana. *Women and Russia.* Boston: Beacon
    Press, 1984.
Massie, Robert K. *Peter the Great, His Life and World.* New
    York: Ballantine Books, 1980.
Massie, Suzanne. *Land of the Firebird.* New York: Simon &
    Shuster, 1980.
Orlova, Raisa. *Memoirs—The Testament of Conscience.* New
    York: Random House, 1983.
Rice, Tamara Talbot. *A Concise History of Russian Art.* Lon-
    don: Thames & Hudson, 1983.
Shevshenko, Arkady N. *Breaking With Moscow.* New York:
    Alfred A. Knopf, 1985.

Shipler, David K. *Russia, Broken Idols, Solemn Dreams.* New York: Time Books, 1983.

Smith, Hedrick. *The Russians.* New York: Ballantine Books, 1977.

Tolstoy, Leo. *War and Peace.* New York: Heritage Press, 1938.

Troyat, Henri. *Catherine the Great.* New York: Berkley Books, 1980.

*Surviving Together, An Update on Soviet/American Relations,* a periodical issued since 1983 by the Friends Committee on National Legislation and the Institute for Soviet-American Relations, Washington, DC.

*Two Soviet Children*

—*photo: Courtesy F.O.R.*